Challenging Your Worldview

Vol. 2

Be Bold

Marcus L. Davis

Challenging Your Worldview Vol. 2 - Be Bold
Copyright© 2025 by Marcus L. Davis.
All rights reserved.

Scripture quotations are from the ESV® Bible (The Holy Bible, English Standard Version®), copyright 2001 by Crossway, a publishing ministry of Good News Publishers. Used by permission. All rights reserved.

THE HOLY BIBLE, NEW INTERNATIONAL VERSION®, NIV® Copyright © 1973, 1978, 1984, 2011 by Biblica, Inc.™ Used by permission. All rights reserved worldwide.

In whole or in part, this publication may not be reproduced, stored in a retrieval system or transmitted, in any form or by any means – electronic, photocopying, mechanical, recording, or otherwise – without express written authorization.

ISBN: 978-1-7378981-2-2 (paperback)

Visit MarcusLDavis.com

Publisher Marcus1Media.com

To my sister, Cheryl.
And to LM, until you understand.
Favored and comforted
to have known both of these women.

I would like to thank you for reading this book, a work written as a letter of love in the key of improvisational living, encouraging all of us to be bold enough to go beyond - until victory.

A portion of the proceeds from this book will go to **affordable housing** causes, and to help the Reflex Sympathetic Dystrophy / Complex Regional Pain Syndrome community (**RSD/CRPS**) causes.

1thousandrocks to take down RSD campaign and support

Thank you!

Contents

Preface: vii

Introduction xv

Chapter 1: Strictly Business— When It's Personal 1

Chapter 2: Your Tomato, My Tomato, or Our Tomatoes 7

Chapter 3: Not My Friend 15

Chapter 4: Marriage—Tying Down the Nuts and Bolts 21

Chapter 5: Anger Soup 33

Chapter 6: The Weight and Blessing of Children 43

Chapter 7: Survive, Alive, or Thrive 51

Chapter 8: You Should Judge Me 63

Chapter 9: Power 69

Chapter 10: Mom, the Unicorn Is Acting Weird 75

Chapter 11: You Need There to Be A God 83

Chapter 12: Truth: The Harsh Lesson 95

A CLOSING REQUEST 101

Topics in Future Volumes 103

Author's Comments: 105

Scripture References by Chapter 107

Preface

How are you doing? I ask this as a well-meaning life coach and mentor with genuine concern. It's likely you picked up this book because you're seeking answers to relationship problems or to break free from the limitations that are stumbling blocks to real success. Your current perspective on the world may be presenting major barriers. This book will help.

But before you delve deeper, I first want to ask you to take a quick self-assessment. Right now, if you'll indulge me, find a mirror and look at yourself with the utmost sincerity. Without focusing on anything negative, ask yourself—physically, mentally, emotionally, and spiritually—"Are my goals for this life lining up with what I truly intend and accept for myself?" Most people's current paths don't reflect the complete fulfillment of all these areas. For that reason, welcome to Be Bold, Volume 2 of the Challenging Your Worldview book series.

In writing this book, my hope for you is that you find the courage to accept how you are doing, and commit to monitoring your well-being regularly. Every so often, ask yourself, "How am I doing?" And give a bold, brazen, and honest answer.

In order to do so, we must consider that life's journey is a compilation of lessons. To provide truly honest feedback about our lives, we need to be self-aware and commit to being lifelong learners. This means we must fully immerse ourselves in what it means to know "how we are doing." The result is greater awareness so that we can contribute to the greatest relationships we can imagine, build, and maintain.

Is this something you want to do? More importantly, is this something you are ready to acknowledge?

Considering what you are learning regarding relationships, you must ask: Do you want to obtain a new level of understanding? To do so, you must give thought to how you decide what you are going to do, how often you are going to do it, and how much time you will allocate to these pursuits. This process formulates your perspective, your mindset—your worldview.

Here is a personal story from my life about a worldview different from the one I possessed. It focuses on my response to an unexpected situation. Living in various cities throughout my life, I experienced something few people do. After finishing a late night breakfast around two or three o'clock in the morning I stumbled upon an obvious societal misdeed.

One of the other restaurant patrons was now outside and standing next to a car with an open trunk. This patron was discussing some business with another man. The second man, who did not enter the restaurant while I was there, stood holding open the trunk of the car. Passing by, alarmed but not shook, I took note of multiple firearms (more than five or ten). The seller noticed me and continued his pitch to the customer without hesitation. The customer did not make any sudden gestures either—as I expected him to. Remembering

Preface

the law enforcement station nearby, I decided to make my way over to it.

But this new station, despite having several marked vehicles in its lot, stood empty. I didn't even see one person guarding the vehicles. My disappointment turned to deciding to do nothing. This was long before mobile phones were popular. Clearly, both the seller and buyer understood that reporting their illegal activities would prove challenging.

That was it. The two criminals from my observation had a worldview that they were not under any stress by a passerby that would cause them to pause. They did not share the same alarm as neither of them knew me or thought they would ever see me again. For them, society posed no threat. Their worldview allowed them to conduct their business openly, confident that circumstances would work in their favor.

Our worldview primarily develops through our early life experiences. Each person encounters different lessons and situations that shape their perspective. From birth until the present moment, life presents countless opportunities for learning and development. Many of us benefit from having someone teach us fundamental life skills—from proper eating habits to social norms that align with our community's values. But, some individuals grow up deprived of essential human experiences like physical affection and loving guidance.

When I was a child, my mother loved to take care of other children. One particular incident stands out in my memory. She once asked a child in her care, "When did someone last give you a hug?" Wow—what a moment! That challenged my worldview and shaped it too. Before that powerful moment, I never considered that other children were not being hugged by their parents. It shocked my young mind. My mother's intuitive understanding amazed me. Sometimes, when I am out and about, I wonder about those basic life skills and human interactions that some children might miss from their parents and how that shapes their worldview.

We do not know when a pearl of wisdom or action such as the aforementioned will strike and impact us. Our worldview is constantly being refined. And I hope you live in such expectation. Welcome true pearls of wisdom from anywhere.

Consider my experience with the first person who discussed Volume 1 of this book series. They approached the conversation eager to challenge the wisdom presented. Their response centered mainly on "What about," "however," and "but" statements. I explained that this precisely illustrated the purpose of our discussion. I asked them to consider: Could there exist a perspective that transcends their current understanding of any subject? A viewpoint that may simultaneously preserve cultural essence or eradicate a cultural mindset if necessary—and yet, enables its evolution? This approach suggests the possibility of creating and revitalizing cultures anywhere, anytime, benefitting everyone involved. The core of accepting better possibilities lies in challenging our established views about relationships. Though initially resistant, this individual gradually gained fresh insights into the content of Volume 1, recognizing its potential to shape a more promising future.

People strive to grasp fundamental concepts to sustain themselves and support their loved ones. This support extends beyond basic necessities like shelter and sustenance to encompass laughter, peace, and health. The pursuit of a brighter future must be linked to a deeper purpose, or it becomes meaningless from the inception. I question whether we express hope genuinely or merely use it as a platitude to help others cope with difficult situations. I use the term "others" because we often allow friends to promote ideals we don't truly embrace (such as guiding your spouse through family trauma).

In relationships, promote only what you genuinely believe. Expressing hope based on universal truths offers more genuine comfort than empty rhetoric (More on hope in chapter 11). People in our lives deserve authentic understanding. I believe this represents the kind of hope you seek as well.

Within marriages and friendships, we seek community to strengthen our beliefs. Constantly introducing doubts and exceptions derails everyone involved. Does this serve any purpose? Your role involves challenging the relationship constructively. Each challenge represents a step forward, followed by another. This sequence of challenges exists because the goal resonates differently with different people. Some grasp it fully, others see it more clearly, while some stand ready to embrace new opportunities. Better still, some people maintain challenging relationships simply to prove their capabilities. Throughout this journey, they discover that true isolation doesn't exist.

I frequently hear people describe undertaking solo ventures or working in isolation. I listen carefully to understand their precise meaning. Usually, their narratives reveal feelings of loneliness rather than true isolation. They rarely acknowledge those who created the tools enabling their achievements. Consider musicians who claim to work alone: they didn't manufacture their instruments, write software, or create their tuning devices. We collaborate with others constantly, whether directly present or not. These indirect connections form part of our shared human experience.

A healthy worldview enables us to manage direct relationships effectively, positively influencing our indirect connections. Pleasant conversation in public spaces creates an environment where families feel welcome, benefitting everyone. When we pollute child-friendly atmospheres with inappropriate or harmful language, we risk perpetuating negative behavior. Our conduct shapes the quality of all relationships, determining our ability to give and receive life's best experiences.

Others will challenge you. They embrace this role as their duty and purpose. Yet, they often miss the crucial point that these challenges reflect more about them than about you. In a world built on mutual exchange, you collaborate with fundamental principles of truth, love, honor, respect, power, and authority. Both parties must work toward compromise. When someone is unwilling to envision a harmonious future together, your challenge shifts. Love persists regardless. You must address these struggles through spiritual warfare while maintaining your personal protection. This includes developing strategies to safeguard those under your care. Community transcends mere discussion – it demands bravery to enhance every relationship.

But what happens when provocations cross into criminal territory? How does your worldview address this? When situations endanger children, what obligations arise? What if your perspective prevents self-reflection and growth? How do you navigate relationships without seeking a more excellent way? Still you speak the truth boldly and clearly (Philippians 3:15).

Preface

As you explore this book, remember that my insights stem from years of helping others overcome challenges. While various experts—pastors, gurus, teachers, therapists, counselors, life coaches, and mentors—offer guidance about life's challenges, you ultimately bear responsibility to become a winner in this life.

To benefit fully from any self-help resource, you must set aside—or at least temporarily suspend—your cultural beliefs, traditions, and established attitudes.

If you resist changing your long-standing behaviors and patterns, no amount of professional guidance—whether from therapists, counselors, gurus, or religious leaders—can facilitate meaningful transformation.

Introduction

If you've read the first volume, you already know that searching for a more excellent way means, "challenging established norms and expectations." To returning readers, and to those joining us for the first time, a warm greeting. In the first volume I laid the foundation giving you the insight to question who is giving you advice and what is the origin of said advice. But growth doesn't stop there—this second volume is here to challenge you even more.

In these pages, we'll build upon the foundational principles from Volume 1 while introducing fresh perspectives that transcend passive knowledge acquisition. On this journey to become more self-aware, it's time for action. For newcomers to my work, rest assured—while this book builds upon its predecessor, it stands independently as a source of transformative insights and paradigm shifts. Nevertheless, I recommend exploring Volume 1 for a more comprehensive understanding.

Throughout this journey, you'll find practical advice, challenges to the status quo and commonplace thinking, and guidance to help you push through to a sustainable way of living. My goal is to make this journey both informative and actionable, so you can start seeing results right away.

So, are you ready to take the next step? Let's begin this introduction by exploring a crucial question.

What is your life being aligned to?

Consider this: when you aspire to a better life, what defines "better" for you? Should your focus be on what is said and written? Whether they come from educators, media personalities, spiritual guides, or the Creator—understanding the distinction between messenger and message reveals the importance of comprehending both. Looking closer at the messenger versus the message indicates the need to connect with both. God is both the Messenger and the Message. A better life means alignment with the original Messenger's intent. Without alignment, you'll always feel misdirected as though something is missing.

Can we imagine that the solutions provided in the message give insight to the messenger? These solutions to our challenges were established before the challenges emerged. Hard to imagine but it is true. God, the Father is loving enough to give us a choice and a solution simultaneously. Our task is to recognize and embrace solutions as timeless as God the Father, acknowledging creation's intentional nature.

No mistake, there is purposeful happenstance (Matthew 5:45). Still there is strict adherence to intentional creation. Each of us has a duty to be aware of this purposeful mandate. It is challenging once you realize you are being aligned. For clarity, consider how our upbringing involved boundaries set by our caregivers. These boundaries challenged our developing minds. Some were flexible, others absolute.

← Introduction →

This raises deeper questions: What underlies these limitations beyond making us good members of society?

To explore this question further, consider this: Are most people leaders or followers? Parents who aspire for their children to become leaders typically do so hoping they'll exercise positive influence rather than becoming a bully. Conversely, for children who tend to follow, parents strive to protect them from being misled. So, what examples are presented for a young mind to follow? It does not matter if you glamorize it or not. If it is attractive to your child (or you), you will find yourself leading or following. A parent has to be willing to ensure the proper things are attractive by what they present. It is incumbent upon us all to remember it is hard to lust after what is not on display. This connects to the emphasis in chapter 6 on engaging with experienced parents to transmit fundamental skills. This early exposure helps shape the mind toward positive patterns.

As stated in Volume 1:

"Critical thinking is needed to work through any situation you may face, positive or negative."

"Challenging Your Worldview drives a particular perspective: everyone seeks advice looking for the best answers to whatever life has for them. Yet the fundamental part of seeking advice is to reconcile the purpose of the advice in the first place."

God's best for a family is both mother and father present in the home, collaboratively engaged and working towards a solid parental structure and children of integrity and positive influence (Proverbs 31). Yes, one person may find themselves alone and dealing with the hardships of taking care of a family. It is still the Creator's original design that supersedes any life challenge we may face. Our role is to be bold enough to accept the Creator's intent despite our circumstances. We must act without transactional idealism. Resilience is a lifestyle of boldness to go beyond the conditions despite how long it takes.

Challenging Your Worldview Volume 2 has three main objectives:

1. Question your personal and public values on different topics to see if they align with one another.

   Be bold enough to take the steps to start now.

2. Redirect your hopes and goals to set them up with a worldview that goes along with what you say and do.

   Today will be tomorrow soon, so utilize today.

3. Arrest your current worldview long enough to think critically about the next chapters in your life. Those who are looking for a better way to understand personal and business relationships will find each chapter in this book to be a highlight of information relevant to now and the future they desire.

   Each time there is a decision to be made, be bold enough to lock into your values.

"Let us therefore come boldly unto the throne of grace, that we may obtain mercy, and find grace to help in time of need." **Hebrews 4:16 (KJV)**

Chapter 1

Strictly Business— When It's Personal

Working outside the home is not the same as working from home. This may seem clear to most people. Still, individuals sometimes lose focus by mixing work scenarios or by the seriousness of their duties both inside and outside the home. Either way, here's a caution for those who fail to take their work duties seriously. "In the name of the Lord Jesus Christ, we command you, brothers and sisters, to keep away from every believer who is idle and disruptive and does not live according to the teaching you received from us" 2 Thessalonians 3:6 (NIV).

Questions:
- How do I protect my family?
- How do I protect my peace?
- Am I the calming voice?

← Challenging Your Worldview →

Life offers too much diversity in people, traditions, and experiences to stay focused on just one thing. Our planet provides countless treasures that make us happy. Visiting the countryside, you might spot wildlife like deer or farm animals. Depending on your geolocation, you could enjoy both snowy mountains or sandy beaches within a few hours' drive. Make a plan, pack up, and head out for a day or two. You and the family will be rewarded.

How do I protect my family?

Each day is an opportunity to increase your family's respect and love for one another. This often requires understanding that workplace issues should stay at work. Or it means being selective about what experiences you share at home.

When your partner works in your field, they might better understand your work challenges. Some partners excel at listening and providing valuable insight when you need it. While this support is valuable, it shouldn't be misused. Family members have boundaries. It's unwise to constantly burden your spouse or child with your professional challenges. Maintain your responsibilities and seek support from professional connections, colleagues, or mentors.

Asking your child's opinion about a product meant for kids, if that's your field, can be valuable. But, avoid mentioning how test groups at work fail to understand your product vision. This may create an unwanted divide between you and your child. Children learn from both our words and actions. Your child might conclude that you look down on other children if they do not understand your full explanation. Pause and ask yourself how much is necessary to share in this instance. Save the rest for a more appropriate audience.

Working in a job field that conflicts with your personal values or preferred practices makes it challenging to leave behind negative industry habits before returning home. Yet, this separation is essential. Create a strategy to process daily challenges, whether through mentor discussions or journal writing. This includes stepping away from toxic situations when needed. There are many industries more inline with what you want to do. It may be a step back. However, it is a step in the right direction.

How do I protect my peace?

Romans 16:17 (ESV) says, "I appeal to you, brothers, to watch out for those who cause divisions and create obstacles contrary to the doctrine that you have been taught; avoid them." Don't you know right from wrong? Doesn't this include your industry's guidelines and accepted practices? The standards you learned when starting your career exist for good reasons. They help keep things orderly, on time, and safe for workers while getting the job done.

The same applies to your home life. If you don't set up rules and order in your home early on, things will get messy and peace will become something you chase instead of something you live. Protecting your peace means knowing when enough is enough and respecting boundaries. At work, you stay away from people who cause trouble and create problems. The same goes for your home. We must learn to navigate the places where you spend most of your time. You want peace. James 3:18 (NIV) says, "Peacemakers who sow in peace reap a harvest of righteousness." It is a way to justify what you say to those around you at work and home.

Unfortunately, your declaration may be met with opposition or even worse, contempt. Remember what Romans 12 teaches us - do your best to live peacefully with everyone. Greet them with a smile and positive energy as much as you can inside your home and everywhere else you go. If you seem unhappy, it shows you're not at peace inside. Saying you've never felt happy is really a cry for help - and it's okay to ask for support. If you have known happiness, share that feeling with others.

In 1 Samuel 25 is a story of David and Abigail and her former husband Nabal - a mean man. According to scripture, David sent friendly greetings to Nabal who rejected the greetings. Eventually, Abigail stepped in to block the death of Nabal at the hands of David; but, Nabal eventually died of a heart attack after learning what happened. Here's something to think about: even if you're unkind like Nabal, you might never know who protected you from harm. By being more peaceful in your daily life, you give others who know you a chance to help you build a better life.

Am I the calming voice?

People's perceptions of your actions can be unpredictable. Some individuals will voice their thoughts, while others stay quiet. A healthy worldview helps form a balanced perspective. Relatives might feel hurt if you skip making the traditional family dish passed down after grandmother's death. To you, it might not seem like a big deal. This time, you decided to experiment with something different for the family gathering. Suddenly, you find yourself in an argument with a relative who claims you never cared about grandma'.

← Strictly Business—When It's Personal →

Unexpectedly, you abandon your character, family bonds become strained, and everything turns deeply personal. Despite the hurt, work to preserve family ties and loving connections. If you need space, take it. When you come back, after emotions have settled, apologize if your words didn't match the person you strive to portray. Be bold enough to apologize to all those who deserve to hear it. Remember, most family members want harmony, not conflict. Also, someone's passing might hold deeper meaning for others than it does for you. James 4:14 (NIV) offers guidance on finding personal peace through these words: "...What is your life? You are a mist that appears for a little while and then vanishes." Do what you can to enjoy your experiences on earth. Be bold enough to be the calming voice.

Chapter 2

Your Tomato, My Tomato, or Our Tomatoes

Creating a society and building social norms is a daunting task, especially when you consider starting an entire nation from scratch. However, the process begins by focusing on a few fundamental needs. These include living quarters, safety of the population, and providing a reliable supply of food, clothing, and transportation. Ultimately, these foundational elements beg the crucial question: who will be in charge of it all?

Questions:
- How do I protect my tomatoes?
- How do I function if no one offers me a hand?
- Am I responsible for correcting oppression?

← Challenging Your Worldview →

Cruising down a deserted highway, dusk settles softly over the landscape. A driver notices her SUV behaving oddly; she pulls over, and discovers an unwelcome screw lodged in her back right tire. Frustrated, she kicks the wheel housing. She looks around and with heightened awareness and reflects on how quickly circumstances can shift in an instant. Is the road hers alone? No, we all share the road. Just at that moment, she sees several trucks parked along an off road and people picking tomatoes.

How do I protect my tomatoes?

Those things seem simple enough when you think of your current worldview. Though it may work for you, do not ignore others who might discover it's not the best approach for keeping your home, society, or nation safe. Let's use the family's food pantry as an example. Think about how you use it. For most of us, it seems simple enough—open the door, retrieve certain items, and close the door. But things get more complex when you realize safety matters both inside and outside your home.

Children, with their innocent intentions, just want something to snack on. But what about your neighbors? Would they help themselves to your supplies if they got the chance? This brings up an important question: Where should you put your pantry? The backyard near the children's play area might sound good, but it's also easily accessible to neighbors.

Working out the details—like how much food to store, security measures, construction plans, or moving the pantry (transportation)—takes careful planning to get right. This is why connecting with others in your community is so valuable. They can help you find the best solutions. Even if you decide to keep it inside your house, remember that children might still find ways to access it - when told not too.

Now, let's think about your personal space, specifically your bedroom. What comes to mind? Most likely comfort, security, and a place to escape where you can truly relax. Comfort is essential in any living space. Making a room truly yours takes time and money, often involving some trial and error. Have you ever purchased a bed only to realize a week later it wasn't right for you? Getting everything just perfect—fromthe bed to the lighting and TV placement—requires time, money, and energy. And it becomes even more challenging when you live with someone who doesn't believe a TV belongs in the bedroom. Comfortable yet?

Discussing bedroom security with your family members is essential. Whether you can afford a separate alarm system for your bedroom or not, you probably have a door that locks. The conundrum presents itself when you note that children need to enter at will and you have a different sleeping schedule from your spouse.

For many people, feeling secure enough to sleep means having proper protection in place. Safeguarding your precious tomatoes (your assets and family) requires adapting to changing circumstances. As we see in so many movies, there can be a bump in the night. The prayer is that it is harmless and of no concern.

You might not regularly encounter situations that remind you of Luke 10:19 (ESV): "Behold, I have given you authority to tread on serpents and scorpions, and over all the power of the enemy, and nothing shall hurt you." But prayer and a Bible-focused life should overcome those things in the spirit. In the physical world, however, security measures are necessary to feel safe and maintain peace of mind. Remember 2 Timothy 1:7 (ESV): "For God gave us a spirit not of fear but of power and love and self-control."

Having important talks with your family about safety is a great idea. Here are some topics to discuss to make sure everyone knows what to do in different situations:

- **What should you do if an intruder gets in?** This is a serious conversation, and it's smart to have a plan. Discuss where to hide, how to call for help, and when it's safe to try to escape.
- **How can you signal for help?** Think about a special signal you can use to let police or trusted neighbors know you need help without making noise. This could be something like flashing a light in a certain pattern or leaving a specific item outside, like a mop. Do this for both adults and children in the home.
- **What situations should you avoid?** Talk about places or times you shouldn't be out alone. For example, walking in a park late at night or going to a party with people you don't know well.
- **What's the plan if you get separated?** If you're at a crowded place like a mall or a fair and get separated, where will you meet? Whom should you call, and where is the alternate contact information located? Discuss a specific meeting spot and a couple of trusted people everyone can call. Having a clear plan can help everyone stay calm and safe.

Be bold enough to protect your home. While we all hope for a peaceful world where such measures aren't needed, being prepared is essential. Creating a secure environment allows you to rest easier, knowing you've taken practical steps to keep your family safe.

How do I function if no one offers me a hand?

The Bible teaches us in Isaiah 1:17 (ESV), "Learn to do good; seek justice, correct oppression; bring justice to the fatherless, plead the widow's cause." Shape your surroundings mindfully; extend kindness to those around you, and watch how it transforms your community's future. Success requires both mental strength (for social connections) and physical energy (for tangible actions). Consider this simple example of moving tomatoes from one place to another.

Getting to a farm where tomatoes are available requires reliable transportation. Whether you're an individual making the trip or a business handling delivery, the process remains the same. We share roadways with our fellow citizens, making life more convenient for everyone. But shouldn't these roads be well-maintained? Absolutely. This is where civic engagement becomes crucial. By respectfully voicing concerns, exercising your right to vote, and fulfilling tax obligations, you earn the right to expect quality infrastructure—well-maintained streets.

Perhaps you're delivering those tomatoes to someone in need who makes that delicious tomato casserole you savor. This exemplifies true community—where people connect and support each other's wellbeing. The expectation of helping neighbors is a necessary norm and is reciprocal. As Acts 4:34 (ESV) reminds us, "There was not a needy person among them, for as many as were owners of lands or houses sold them and brought the proceeds of what was sold."

Sometimes you might find yourself isolated, with no one available to deliver a basket of freshly picked tomatoes. Still, as hard as it can seem for you at the moment, reach out to others. Your willingness to collaborate with others does go a long way. And as the saying goes, a tomato saved is a tomato earned. Not really. The saying does go differently. And the thought needs updating to something like this: "If you share a tomato with a friend today, it is an investment in a tomato for tomorrow." Is what you are able to do today, at the expense of tomorrow?

Am I responsible for correcting oppression?

Consider your tomato and my tomato. What is the benefit if we all share our tomatoes? Is there enough to go around? A viable society understands that some people will inevitably have more tomatoes than others.

Look at human history. Doesn't it show us this pattern? We can move forward knowing that no one has to face life's challenges alone unless they demand it. But choosing to stand alone requires having enough resources—the strength to carry your message of being alone, food for energy, and protection from life's storms. Do you want to stand alone in the rain?

When people try to break away from society and its opportunities, they often discover they miss their place in it. And when you get back into the flow of society it might be challenging for you. Remember, it's also challenging for others who have continued their journey. Sometimes, a fresh start in a new place—whether it's another part of your country or a completely different nation—can help you find a farm where you can pick better tomatoes.

We're stronger and better together. Building a powerful community starts with recognizing that everyone has something worthwhile to share. This applies to our families, neighborhoods, towns, states or commonwealth. We're better as one—especially when we're committed to working together. This is a worldview worth protecting.

It's about reaching out to help others when they're struggling, cultivating a culture of mutual support, and working toward goals that benefit everyone. When we isolate ourselves and refuse to share our gifts, we contribute to a fractured society.

Your neighbors have something to share with you, just as you have something to share with them. If we work to build the roads together we can sell our tomatoes together. As a society, we ask of one another that no one cripples the ability of another in their healthy pursuits. Naturally, some of us will sell more tomatoes. It is okay as long as their worldview bears in mind this important message: "Woe to those who plan iniquity, to those who plot evil on their beds! At morning's light they carry it out because it is in their power to do it. They covet fields and seize them, and houses, and take them. They defraud people of their homes, they rob them of their inheritance." (Micah 2:1-2, NIV).

Others will figure out that their lot in life is to build the roads for trucks carrying local produce. The varying talents of our collective efforts benefit us all. And we must be bold enough to remember that some of us are likely to crush the less fortunate. While no society is perfect, we must fight against unfairness using shared values like this:

"A ruler who oppresses the poor is like a driving rain that leaves no crops" (Proverbs 28:3, NIV).

In the grand scheme of society, every individual, like a ripe tomato, has something valuable to offer. By sharing our abundance and working in harmony, we can ensure that no one is left behind. A proper worldview joins hands, builds bridges, and cultivates a society where everyone has the chance to flourish. Together, we can sow the seeds of a brighter future. We govern ourselves best when we are aware that your tomato is my tomato; it ensures we produce more tomatoes for us all (Matthew 22:39 and Mark 12:31).

Chapter 3

Not My Friend

A friend can drift in and out of your life freely. Unlike the permanent bonds of blood relations, friendships often maintain a natural boundary. Yet sometimes, these connections deepen into something more profound—like blood kinship. Whether through conscious choice or the natural evolution of shared experiences, friends can transform into family. All of us must recognize clearly when this shift occurs. It means they have become as essential to you as you are to them. While we sometimes distance ourselves from obtuse relatives, we must consider if friendship-turned-family bonds deserve the same treatment.

Questions:
- How do my closest friends categorize me?
- Am I able to forgive family and forgive friends?
- Is Jesus my friend?

← Challenging Your Worldview →

As you walk down the street you spot someone you haven't seen since your later high school days. You knew this person before you ventured off to the military, college, or for a career elsewhere. They see you, wave, and make their way over to your favorite spot in town. You exchange hello's. As they are speaking you remember this person was just someone you vaguely knew but spent time with due to shared classes. You allow them to reminisce, and then you expect them to be on their way. But they stick around a little longer, and the unfortunate life they have led, since you saw them last, starts to unfurl like a carpet.

How do my closest friends categorize me?

You probably realize, I care as a fellow human being but I really have nothing to offer that will have an impact. Then you remember this passage from Luke 11:5-7 (NIV) it says: "Suppose you have a friend, and you go to him at midnight and say, 'Friend, lend me three loaves of bread; a friend of mine on a journey has come to me, and I have no food to offer him.' And suppose the one inside answers, 'Don't bother me. The door is already locked, and my children and I are in bed. I can't get up and give you anything.'" Now you are the friend inside with the door locked. Do you in fact have something to offer? Although this is not someone who you consider to be family, you have something that is invaluable. Your advice and presence can make a difference in the person's life.

All of your friends, especially your closest friends, hope that you would offer something if needed. Does this match what they expect from you? If not, what gives? Are you even a casual friend to anyone? A shared experience that reflects on society means a stranger should receive something of value. Being a listening ear is important for those

← Not My Friend →

who are familiar with your presence. Even more so for those who know you, being there to listen makes a significant difference.

Take a moment to list your closest friends—up to seven individuals who truly matter in your life. Don't worry if your list is shorter; research shows many people maintain fewer than five intimate friendships, some even fewer than three. If you're fortunate enough to have seven close friends, acknowledge them all.

Next, identify your five core behavioral patterns—those instinctive responses that emerge during both peace or crisis. For example: The willingness to drive anywhere at any time or the offering of a listening ear until the friend feels heard. For friends that treat you like family, can they depend on your consistent character and reactions?

Joyful moments and peaceful times often bring people together to share experiences. Crisis may be the only time you may see other friends. They are there for you, supportive with resources, and follow up when necessary. Have you considered if these same people would include you among their closest friends? Can others count on you during both tough times and happy occasions? It is a challenge to accept that your friends may handle relationships differently from how you do (or plan to). It can be eye-opening.

Our view of close friends should change when we consider the following passages: "Do not make friends with a hot-tempered person, do not associate with one easily angered" (Proverbs 22:24 NIV), and "The righteous choose their friends carefully, but the way of the wicked leads them astray" (Proverbs 12:26 NIV). Be bold enough to wait patiently to see if your newly minted friendship reveals someone who defends you when you are not around and, even better, they bolster your name. A proper worldview of a good friend is someone who markets your character even when not in your presence.

Now, a reality check. Perhaps your personality isn't something to celebrate or admire. Yet, you remain a valuable friend to have. If this describes you, summon the courage to transform. If this describes your friends, be bold enough to evaluate who truly belongs in your inner circle. What message do you want to convey about the company you keep? Remember, it's perfectly acceptable to evolve beyond relatives and friends who don't share the healthiest worldview that aligns with your personal standards and the expectations you hold for those closest to you.

Am I able to forgive family and forgive friends?

We often rush to make judgments with others before understanding the complete picture. Proverbs 18:13 (NIV) helps us focus: "To answer before listening— that is folly and shame." In other words, making quick judgments without knowing all facts is foolishness. Sometimes friendships sail smoothly without being tested between loyalties to family or other friends. That's a blessing. Part of a peaceful life means never experiencing broken bonds. Remarkably, some relationships grow stronger after facing challenging situations. Consider yourself fortunate if you find a friend with such depth of character at any stage of friendship. Thank God.

When someone's actions hurt you deeply or a friend's behavior seems untrustworthy, take time to process. Remember that every friend, like you, is walking their own path of personal development. Hopefully, they recognize their own need for improvement. Don't badger them to change or rush their progress. Focus on being your best self, and in areas where you need growth, perhaps they can inspire you with their example.

Psalm 109:4 (NIV) teaches, "In return for my friendship they accuse me, but I am a man of prayer." Love them no matter what; this means you are willing to forgive their indiscretions. Whether these wrongs affect you personally, your inner circle, or complete strangers. Let me be clear about a healthy worldview. Protect yourself from being prey even while you pray. Remain vigilant against becoming vulnerable. Certain friendships may require establishing strict boundaries due to their behavior. Continue praying for these individuals, thank God for them, and appreciate God's work that enables you to forgive and move forward (Philippians 1:3-6, NIV).

Is Jesus my friend?

James 4:4 (NIV) strikes a chord with this passage: "You adulterous people, don't you know that friendship with the world means enmity against God? Therefore, anyone who chooses to be a friend of the world becomes an enemy of God." Ouch! That verse stings. And it makes you question what is "the world"? In short, it means hostility towards the morality and orderliness of God. Our command as believers (or not) is certainly not to engage with immorality. I know many atheists who believe in some form of morality, even if it is askew and/or borrowed from God.

A worldview that promotes harmony must have morality. How can we expect tranquility in a society that has abandoned the fundamental principle shared across many cultures—showing compassion and respect for others? It's a simple formula for living harmoniously. A mindset that changes that, and makes most people in the culture leave a compassionate and respectful worldview is not a friend of God. Such individuals worship wealth and material possessions, believing these make them better than others less privileged. Power is not the goal but the crown God provides for a job well done.

In the book of John 15:15 (ESV), Jesus says "No longer do I call you servants, for the servant does not know what his master is doing; but I have called you friends, for all that I have heard from my Father I have made known to you." That is comforting. The Creator of the heavens and earth considers you a friend. It is contingent upon your rejecting the hostile world and accepting His principles to include Christ. There are two simple guidelines. In brief they exclaim: Love God, and love your neighbor as yourself (Mark 12).

Be bold enough to be a supportive friend who forgives and offers wise direction to others. In order to do that you must show presence to casual acquaintances and close friends. Such actions strengthen our community bonds. When you listen attentively to others, you gain valuable insights that may benefit someone else in your inner circle one day. Whether it's extending forgiveness, sharing resources, donating to those in need, demonstrating humility, lending your car, or offering assistance, these actions form the foundation of meaningful friendships. Doing such things shows friendliness and is a proper worldview in light of Jesus' teachings. Jesus spoke concerning friendship with himself as a proper worldview: "Whoever hates me hates my Father also", John 15:23 (ESV).

Chapter 4

Marriage—Tying Down the Nuts and Bolts

Marriage enriches society and humanity as a whole. Let's explore this deeper connection. Your heart's closest companion follows a sacred order. First comes your spiritual relationship with Jesus; next is the one you share your bed with; which is your spouse, followed by your children, and finally your neighbors and community. This aligns with the fundamental principles of love, honor, and respect as taught in the two commandments (Mark 12:30-31).

Accepting the above paragraph allows a relationship to evolve the physical into its proper form: a spiritual bond. That is why you become one with your spouse (Matthew 19:5). Yet the challenge remains: "One person is invigorated with cleaning the house and ready to take on the day, the other is ready to go back to bed."

Questions:
- What advice should a marriage get from other couples?
- What are some important points for couples to consider?
- Who or what is the final answer on marriage advice?

"I do not want to be married any longer. It is time to unboard this train at the next stop. I am out of here." Is that your frame of reference anytime things become difficult? Have you heard the only reason Jesus allows for divorce is infidelity (Matthew 19)? It is important to note that Jesus goes on to explain living without being married is sometimes a choice and there is a challenge of becoming one with your spouse. Matthew 19:11 (NIV) says, "...Not everyone can accept this word, but only those to whom it has been given."

What advice should a marriage get from other couples?

Bible is an instruction book on how to obtain wisdom. One, ask God the Creator who instituted marriage. Two, talk to others in the same predicament or formerly in the same predicament with success on the other side (be mindful about what you share or follow). What you choose to follow has consequences. And, you will live with it even if you do not like the ideas presented.

Here are some key factors to consider as you seek advice from other married couples.

1. Is this the right couple? Advice for righteous living is necessary; but, the choice of advisor can lead you down the wrong path. Remember it is natural for people to take sides—based on age, similitude, gender or attraction.
2. Strongly consider any advisor's intentions. Do they really have your best interest at heart? Don't just unload your complete marriage picture on them. Take a breath and ask questions.

← Tying Down the Nuts and Bolts →

One really good question to ask the man is this: "Why are you still married to her after the children left home?" And for the wife, ask this: "Other than the Bible what is your main source of wisdom?" After asking, wait for a satisfactory answer.

3. If there is a major age, cultural, or regional difference in your marriage versus the couple offering advice, do you still listen?
4. Can they provide Biblically sound wise counsel concerning coitus?
5. Are you secure enough to be vulnerable in front of others? Do not wait until your marriage is in serious trouble to become vulnerable.

The way you process and embrace their guidance rests in your hands as someone seeking help. As you build the foundation of your personal perspective, you must determine what matters most. The advisors sharing their wisdom deserve your consideration, particularly when fees are involved. Feel empowered to examine their perspectives and intentions. Keep in mind you're sharing your deepest relationship concerns about your chosen partner. Don't treat this casually just because other couples show interest in your situation.

One life coach shared that he once had nefarious intentions by attempting to sabotage a couple's relationship, hoping to pursue the wife afterward. While seeking advice about personal matters is perfectly acceptable, failing to evaluate crucial life decisions thoroughly can lead to regret.

Remember, your life partner stands beside you during life's most heart-wrenching moments—whether it's grieving a parent's passing, celebrating financial victories or calamities, or enduring the unthinkable. Take time to deeply consider both your partner's true character and the integrity of those offering relationship advice. Their values will impact your journey.

What are some important points for couples to consider?

When you say "I do," remember this truth: Your partner will evolve. Time will bring inevitable transformations. Their dietary choices, fashion sense, physical appearance, knowledge base, social circles, life goals, career aspirations, and most importantly, their feelings toward you—all will undergo metamorphosis. Are you prepared for this journey?

Life's dynamics shift with time. And from your perspective it may get better or worse. Accepting that various aspects of your relationship will transform at different speeds is essential wisdom that couples must embrace with patience.

Exchange with your future spouse a list of five essential elements you each need for a fulfilling marriage. Create your own list, too, and share them openly. Remember that while your top three priorities tend to remain stable, the fourth and fifth elements often fluctuate more as life unfolds. You and/or your spouse may not adhere to the lesser points.

You are fortunate if you experience six or seven years of uninterrupted bliss. It is a blessing. Life brings various obstacles and transformations along the way. As a woman, are you ready to embrace the Biblical teaching of respecting your husband's leadership (Ephesians 5:22)? And husbands, will you do your part? Show understanding toward your wives and cherish them as your own body

← Tying Down the Nuts and Bolts →

(1 Peter 3:7, Ephesians 5:28-29). Remember, men: Your physical self belongs to your wife. Are you prepared to share with her everything you do with "her body" (Mark 10:7-8)? For those who follow Christ and read these words, are you ready to stand before God with your response?

Consider the following when you are looking to be married (or are already married):

1. What does blissful marriage mean to me? What does blissful marriage mean to my spouse? As time progresses decade upon decade, how might these definitions evolve and transform?
2. What are the code words for giving me space, and what is the amount of time I need? Define your definition of "space" (1 Corinthians 7:5)? We focus on the physical because of our culture and natural instincts. Bear in mind, however, that your partner's essence extends far beyond their physical attributes.
3. Given that many cultures believe that arguing is inevitable, what is off limits? Many couples will often state the word "divorce" can never be uttered during a passionate debate (Matthew 19, Genesis 2).
4. Detail what discussions are off the table during date night or breakfast)—children, inlaws, work, money (decide who pays before the date), or house chores?

Here are some suggestions to excite your conversation: travel, hobbies, faith, history, origins of your political stances, books, family security, other places to go for a date, movies,

← Challenging Your Worldview →

architecture, trucks, and comedy. May I suggest, be a full person to your spouse.

5. Have you committed to your shared journey, both present and future? What happens when life's purpose evolves; will your union remain possible? Keep in mind that partnerships are never, if ever 50/50. Today's balance may feel perfect, but circumstances shift. For example, what if we need to care for aging parents.

6. Address these important points through open dialogue:
   a) We're having this discussion because of our deep commitment to each other.
   b) While marriage talks can be difficult, we are determined to succeed. Let's agree to forgive each other before tackling these challenging conversations.
   c) We'll honor each other's perspectives. Truth comes from recognizing God's guidance, not from self-righteousness.
   d) Our extended family and children will see us as a united front and respect us as a couple.
   e) Approach these talks with openness to both learn and teach, serving your spouse and strengthening your bond. *Discuss one topic at a time until its conclusion.*
   f) Before starting, let's clearly outline what we want to achieve. Keep it simple.
   g) It's okay to say: "I don't know my answer to that right now." or "Can I think about my answer and get back to you?"

7. Remember, both of you have a lifelong vested interest in the success of your marriage.

◀— **Tying Down the Nuts and Bolts** —▶

a) Eliminating detrimental surprises by sharing deep family secrets.

b) Maintain a certain distance from co-workers, family members, and friends. The two of you becoming one is primary to any other human connection.

Break time—a lot to digest if you are taking these points seriously. Take a moment, ponder for a few weeks and write the answers. You do not have to keep the answers. Writing them is just to help you organize your conclusions, find supporting materials, and advice to advance the best marriage possible for you and your family. If you do not know what you feel about a situation or want regarding how to move forwards, say so.

Now for a few more:

8. What am I willing to give up to maintain my life in Christ with my spouse?
9. What are we allowed to share with friends?
10. How often will I revisit my understanding of my spouse and myself to ensure the healthiest marriage because neither one of us is of greater value?
11. Do I have any history of triggers, stressors or historical events that are problematic, such as:
    a) lack of money/debt
    b) planning life events
    c) parenting phobias
    d) procrastination
    e) minimalist or luxury lifestyle (which is a deal breaker?)
    f) shopping/spending money as therapy
    g) how are we handling banking

h) family money versus extended family money.

What should my spouse know about me given that they are a life partner? Do not expect your spouse to be your counselor or therapist. If they are, what happens when you heal *(or if you don't)*? It is okay if you do not know the answers to these questions. It is the reason to openly communicate with a mentor and your life partner.

12. How often will we discuss Bible principles together?
13. How often will we pray as a couple?
14. How often do we pray as a family with the children?
15. Who will be the main point of contact for the following (a different responsibility does not mean someone is of greater or lesser value than the other):
    a) Family health?
    b) Family spiritual health?
    c) Family prayer life and putting into practice Biblical principles?
    d) Family provider—the one who maintains their job for the good of the family?
    e) Sacrificing their job for the good of the family?
    f) Family home (the building)?
    g) Family finances, ambitions, and goals?

Men, depending on your culture and region of the world, it is likely that you are the head of the family either through providing, subjection, or tradition. Either way, it is important to note this passage: "But I want you to understand that the *head of every man is Christ*, the head of a wife is her husband, and the head of Christ is God" (1st Corinthians 11:3, ESV). With patient mercy, love and understanding may the grace of God offer you the wisdom and boldness to accept that as true. You have a direct connection and a direct responsibility (1 Peter 3:7).

Who or what is the final answer on marriage advice?

Does giving advice have a premise? From professional advisors like therapists, spiritual leaders, and educators to personal connections like family members and colleagues, everyone seems ready to share their wisdom. But who can truly guide you toward the right path? More important, have you considered how their personal experiences and cultural beliefs shape their advice? This means their worldview.

All ideas should be calibrated with one focus in mind: Success in Christ. Otherwise it is null and void for a true marriage.

The ideal candidate for your marriage partner is one who carries most similar beliefs and has a basis for those beliefs. Mommy and daddy said so—is not good enough. What backs up those ideals from the parents and beyond that? Is the advice timeless (Ephesians 5:31)? Too many parents have great intentions and may have tremendous insight. Use it to discover other mentors who have insight for a Biblical worldview of marriage.

The Bible teaches, "For by wise guidance you can wage your war, and in abundance of counselors there is victory" Proverbs 24:6 (ESV).

Let's face it. "Many counselors" in marriage guidance focus on marketing products, courses, and workshops. When seeking direct guidance, keep it simple—just the couple and a trusted advisor, coach, or therapist. Do not misunderstand me; all of the aforementioned products may have tremendous value. But, all of it should funnel back to you as a couple and one mentor. Multiple counselors often give conflicting advice. How do you determine which path to take when every suggestion appears valid? God through prayer and you as a couple talking honestly with one marriage mentor. Tell the mentor everything you are learning from different publications and seminars.

Here is an example. Earlier in this chapter we discussed the only reason for breaking up a marriage according to Jesus' teachings. Does that mean if your spouse displays unbearable behavior you cannot divorce? As you seek advice, keep in mind their source of information concerning the above sentence. You may find that many advisors use culture, traditions, and personal experience. Those can be highlighted to ensure relevance to your needs. However, principles never change.

What in your vows covered lying, drunkenness, financial ruin, etc., that you did not mean when you agreed for better or for worse? If a (spiritually) sick person needs help, what is the case for turning your back on them? Help them and *protect yourself*. And love them from afar. That does not mean divorce if what Jesus portrays is accurate. For better or worse means you decided on your wedding day you would get them help for whatever comes. There is a lot more to say concerning this that should take place outside the pages of this book. *Marriage is not something to take lightly* (Matthew 19:8-12). Pray and allow the word of God to reform the hardness of our collective hearts.

It is likely you may never have heard it explained that way before in your circle, at your church or from your spiritual leader. Following God is the highest form of self protection. Reverence for God in your marriage means you do not pacify dysfunction. Study it. Be bold enough to follow up.

◄— **Tying Down the Nuts and Bolts** —►

Now that you know you are turning your marriage over to the Messiah, the Holy One of God, the Most High—Jesus the Christ—how is that done at this point going forward? The previous paragraphs highlight why couples need guidance before marriage and continued support afterward. The blending of different cultural backgrounds creates unique challenges that deserve careful attention and wisdom.

Growing up in the same neighborhood, two houses apart, going to the same schools; and still, what is happening inside their home is not the same as yours. Success is a journey that takes time and patience. And just as countless others have done it, so can you. That is good news.

When your partner suggests counseling, either before or after marriage, gently ask them to share their perspective on counseling—not your particular need, just their perspective. Stay open and non-defensive in your approach. Give them space to express their thoughts without interruption. Could their suggestion be coming from a place of wanting to build a stronger, more fulfilling relationship with you?

The principles of a good worldview for marriage are illustrated in the Bible. If your mentor is not Biblically sound and willing to show you in the scripture the context for their beliefs, strongly consider another mentor. Yet mentorship is worthless and their technique is futile if you both are dishonest. Also consider if you desire a marriage that honors God versus one that honors yourself and tradition.

Chapter 5

Anger Soup

Slow to speak?! Not a chance when this person makes me so angry. Does that mean you are at the whim of another? Have you tried to make yourself angrier? Does it mean the destruction of something or someone? Let's take a breath before we go further into this challenge about anger.

As a minister (or life coach), please understand that this book does not serve as a medical treatment or diagnostic tool. If you're dealing with, causing, or putting upon others any anger issues that require immediate attention, please seek help right away. Don't hesitate to visit a medical facility or dial 911 if needed. This chapter focuses on examining and challenging your perspectives about anger - exploring whether it serves any valuable purpose in your life.

Questions:
- Who requires that you become angry?
- Does my anger have to do with expectations?
- Is there a purpose for anger?

The impact of losing a cherished grandmother varies significantly based on our age and emotional maturity. Think of a young child of six, whose precious memories revolve around simple joys like Grandma's embrace and baking together. Their grief manifests in straightforward questions like "Why did Grandma have to go?"

Compare this to an eighteen year-old who experienced a more complex bond—sharing life's wisdom, embarking on memorable travels, and receiving promises of support in higher education. Their emotional response is more intricate, built on years of meaningful connections. The elder-teen recalls Grandma's guidance with schoolwork, presence at important events, and unwavering support during tough times.

When both siblings transition to living with an unfamiliar uncle (despite his sincere efforts), their grief manifests differently because their experiences and grasp of loss differ fundamentally.

Who requires that you become angry?

Let's explore a fundamental question: Who requires that you become angry? Think about it carefully. While some societies effectively guide disruptive emotions into constructive outlets like sports or art, others carelessly promote anger without considering its harmful effects on everyone involved. Just because your cultural background might view angry outbursts as a sign of strength or masculinity doesn't make them emotionally healthy. Even when anger appears protective, like defending loved ones, it becomes problematic if it doesn't teach anything valuable or lead to personal growth. It's simply raw emotion without purpose. So, I ask you again to reflect deeply: Who actually requires you to become angry?

Here is another question I want you to weigh with careful consideration. Is there a particular person pressuring you to feel angry? It could be a relative who assumes you'll share in their emotions. Maybe you feel a spiritual obligation to be angry about unfairness in the world. Consider honestly: What authority did you give these individuals or influences over your emotional state? If you know they don't truly control you, why allow their expectations to determine your feelings?

Sacred anger is known as righteous indignation. It provides direction and understanding, eliminating any chance for resistance. This is exemplified by the great flood narrative in Genesis.

All of humanity is given a choice when you consider this passage from James 1:19-20 (ESV): "My dear brothers and sisters, take note of this: Everyone should be quick to listen, slow to speak and slow to become angry because human anger does not produce the righteousness that God desires." For followers of God, this wisdom should resonate deeply. Those who do not, ask yourselves whether the anger requirement is useful or harmful. The answer becomes clear through quiet reflection: When we allow others to trigger our anger, who bears the cost? The physical toll of suppressed rage, the damage to our relationships, and the ripple effects through our community fall squarely on us. By letting others dictate our emotional state, we surrender far too much of our personal power.

When you pause to reflect deeply on this matter, and ask ourselves, "What forces you to react with anger?" This doesn't address this universal human challenge. You must first recognize that you face a choice between responding with anger or "turning the other cheek." When others disrespect your boundaries, possessions, requirements, and family, taking the peaceful route becomes more challenging. Yet, choosing not to react with anger helps you realize that those trying to provoke you may not have your best interest at heart. They may want to see destruction to prove their personal malice against you or the group they have decided you belong to that is unsavory.

Never surrender your emotional control to others. Question their motives. "Are they genuinely concerned for your wellbeing when they stir up your anger?" The aforementioned wisdom from James's teachings emphasizes the importance of being patient and attentive before giving in to anger, reminding all of us that acting in anger doesn't align with God's purpose for our lives.

Reclaim authority over your emotional responses from everyone—whether it's strangers, workplace associates, cultural pressures, friends, or family. While this isn't simple, especially if you're used to reactive patterns, be bold enough to embrace a new perspective that serves your desired life better and causes less harm. Yes, it requires consistent practice.

Does my anger have to do with my expectations?

Let me ask you something. How do you envision your day unfolding when you wake up? Do you anticipate kindness or blatant disrespect? It's mentally draining to start your day expecting negativity after peaceful rest. We each hold unique views on respect. The standards shift between public spaces and our private sanctuary. Therefore, what I envision for my day may have to do with where I intend to go.

When we lash out at people, we're essentially demanding, "You must think and act exactly like I would." Perhaps we feel entitled to special consideration—respect, understanding, and admiration from those around us.

Consider this everyday scenario. When another driver suddenly swerves into our lane cutting us off, we react with frustration, thinking, "I would never drive so carelessly!" We judge harshly, forgetting one crucial fact—their perspective differs from ours.

From a Biblical perspective, we understand that God's anger is unique. It perfectly balances righteousness and grace. This explains why the concept of forgiveness extends beyond our conscious transgressions to include those we commit unknowingly. This divine mercy covers even the deepest offenses against our Creator, sins whose magnitude is beyond our full comprehension.

Genesis opens with "In the beginning God created…" revealing a purposeful Creator. Consider this: You've meticulously cleaned your vehicle that you purchased through hard work, and your teenage driver, newly licensed, has just had an accident. You provided all the necessary guidance, showed understanding, offered practice sessions, and ultimately extended trust by allowing your child to drive independently.

What were your hopes? Certainly not an accident. Does this situation warrant pure anger or justified disappointment? The latter becomes appropriate if you know your child fully understood vehicle control and speed limitations but chose to ignore them.

We understand that anger serves no purpose unless we transform it into a learning opportunity for personal development. In our daily interactions, we must recognize that everyone has their own identity. They have different perspectives and experiences that make them who they are. Consider that traffic scenario again. Even when a young driver understands traffic regulations, responding with pure rage won't improve their driving habits. Did you previously have a positive influence on that young person? Will your brand of anger break that bond? Justified disappointment means providing appropriate consequences to the teen. Off-brand anger (going overboard with anger) may break the bond.

Think about another motorist. The person who swerved in front of you isn't aware that your special occasion cake got damaged when you hit the brakes hard. They're consumed by their own challenges, concerns, and destination. Here's another perspective: Can you be certain they noticed your vehicle? Are you aware if their vehicle is properly maintained? Could they be responding to an urgent situation?

What if we channeled anger into understanding? God's example shows us this transformative approach. When God teaches about anger, it guides us toward compassion and mutual respect. Bear in mind there is a difference in God's judgment and human to human judgement as expressed in Romans 1:18-20, Romans 12:17-21, and Matthew 18:15-17. Anger is not a reason to relinquish your responsibility or concern for others until the person makes it clear they do not have a worldview of personal growth. (More about judgment in chapter 8).

The unreasonableness of anger can change your reality in an instant. Have you considered how presumptuous it is to demand that others align with your perspective? When your temper subsides and clarity returns—restoring your faith in a harmonious worldview — does your mindset shift? Do those heated thoughts retain their validity, or do they appear less justified when examined through the calm light of reason?

People will present countless triggers for your anger. Choose your reactions thoughtfully. Know that disrespect will come your way, sometimes deliberately, other times thoughtlessly. This isn't about pardoning such conduct. Rather, it's worth reflecting on this wisdom from Ephesians 4:31 (NIV): "Get rid of all bitterness, rage and anger, brawling and slander, along with every form of malice." This teaching doesn't imply these emotions are simple to manage, but rather highlights their destructive nature and worth working to overcome.

Is there a purpose for anger?

Ecclesiastes 7:9 (NIV) says, "Do not be quickly provoked in your spirit, for anger resides in the lap of fools." This wise teaching from Solomon teaches us that rushing to anger reveals poor emotional intelligence. When we allow our feelings to hijack our responses, we lose the opportunity for mindful reflection and balanced reactions. Similar to how a fool makes snap judgments without proper evaluation, those who let anger surge too quickly often face the consequences of their hasty reactions.

How do we proceed using a purposeful worldview? Surround yourself with people who do not bolster angry feelings. For some, this might seem impossible. Or your surroundings may demand self-preservation measures. Allow your anger to serve only two purposes: righteous guidance and self-defense. God's guidelines are displayed as principles and discipline. God's protection is the destruction of sinfulness and those who champion it.

In your relationships, "Do not make friends with a hot-tempered person, do not associate with one easily angered, or you may learn their ways and get yourself ensnared" (Proverbs 22:24, NIV). This practical advice warns us about the company we keep. Just like catching a cold from someone who's sick, we can "catch" bad anger habits from people who can't control their temper.

This practical advice from the Bible guides us in selecting our social circle. Like catching a virus from someone who's ill, we can absorb unhealthy emotional responses from people who struggle with a heated temperament. The verse uses the word "ensnared"—like getting caught in a trap—to show how dangerous it is to copy someone else's anger patterns. Focus your energy on positive relationships and strategies to connect with individuals who demonstrate emotional intelligence and a healthy worldview.

Emotions like anger work as internal messengers—your body's natural alert system. When anger surfaces, it's highlighting an issue that requires your conscious attention before it escalates. But just like a warning light on the car's dashboard doesn't resolve the issue, experiencing anger won't fix your challenges. Rather, let it be your guide to deeper self-awareness, helping you identify what needs transformation and how to achieve it mindfully.

Feeling entitled to respect is rational, especially concerning neighbors. Yet, this desire can become excessive. But when frustration builds, it may transform into deliberate hostility and a wish to hurt others. This mindset serves no one well. The key lies in channeling your emotions differently. Can you be bold enough to use that energy to build bridges instead of walls with your neighbors? That is a

Anger Soup

healthier worldview. If the elderly neighbor's yard is a problem, offer to help with the yard work or assist them with cleaning their driveway.

Nevertheless, that powerful sensation of frustration, resentment, threat or antagonism—anger—persists. The wise perspective isn't to eliminate anger completely. Rather, it's to recognize anger's value and appropriate role in our lives.

We must recognize, however, that others may be indifferent to our anger. Consider: do you typically concern yourself with another person's anger? Generally, the answer is negative (unless you perceive a direct threat to yourself).

"Fathers, do not exasperate your children; instead, bring them up in the training and instruction of the Lord," states Ephesians 6:4 (NIV). When parents provoke anger in their children towards themselves or society, they force their children to spend excessive time healing emotional or physical wounds inflicted upon themselves, family, relationships, and community.

Be bold enough to seek wisdom and admit, "I'm uncertain about my needs; I'm here with an open mind, ready to learn and take positive action."

Chapter 6

The Weight and Blessing of Children

Do these thoughts echo in your mind: "How do I handle this child?" Or perhaps you've muttered, "If only kids came with an instruction manual." And this classic, "My other children were a breeze to raise, but this one? So challenging, despite using the same parenting approach."

Take comfort in knowing you're not walking this challenging parenting journey alone. And here's a vital truth to embrace: Letting your child experience both success and failure(redirection) is essential for their growth.

Questions:
- What are some main principles if there isn't one book to use?
- When do I let go?
- How do I communicate the unknown?

Entering into marriage creates a unique partnership built on: Some level of mutual understanding and reasoning is essential. However, becoming a parent means forming a bond with someone who might one day resent you or hold negative feelings towards you. And, the weight of parenthood becomes especially apparent during those challenging teenage years.

Yet, there's joy in watching a person's life unfold and witnessing their journey of self-discovery. It's deeply rewarding (even more so with your spouse) to observe which experiences shape them into compassionate individuals. Whether they find purpose in serving the elderly, technology or pursue a career in transportation, life often takes unexpected turns. Our initial expectations rarely match the final outcome. But mentoring, nurturing and shaping the mind of another person is pure joy.

What are some main principles if there isn't one book to use?

Anyone can cite psychological studies and scientific findings. While these perspectives may offer valuable insights through their unique lens, they remain theoretical until put into practice. Take note of recurring themes and principles in different publications throughout history.

Here are some helpful principles you'll discover:
1. Create space for children to express themselves freely. Although you still have to guide them in understanding personal boundaries as they develop.

2. Encourage them to revisit familiar healthy environments, which strengthens their confidence and enhances recall.
3. Introduce controlled changes to foster a growth mindset. For instance, occasionally walk with your child to school instead of taking their usual bus route. Of course, it is important that you avoid disrupting routines that could cause psychological harm.
4. Create chances for them to plan celebrations for others and experience being celebrated themselves. Vary the use of significant expenses or public displays for these celebrations.
5. Support their curiosity to explore nature, cultural institutions, lakes & rivers, literature, and celestial objects.

This compilation isn't exhaustive of all principles. Rather, it serves as a mirror to reflect where you stand in your parenting worldview. Effective implementation of any parenting philosophy requires honest self-assessment of your growth as a caregiver and your impact on those under your guidance.

The Bible teaches in Titus 2 that women who practice sound doctrine are to teach younger women. The focus lies in sharing everyday wisdom. Picture bringing your baby home, only to discover you're facing a challenging diaper rash with no experienced parent to consult. What seemed like a straightforward situation suddenly becomes an overwhelming moment of uncertainty.

Building a support network is essential in child-rearing. When family isn't available, the local church is a place to start. This naturally brings up the concept of trust, highlighting the importance of fostering positive relationships with those around us. As these connections grow stronger, they create safe spaces for open dialogue and genuine interactions.

Reflecting on Titus 2:6's wisdom: "...Encourage the young men to be self-controlled." In societies where male leadership is traditional, practicing self-restraint becomes crucial. Remember, male behavior often sets the tone for female responses. This understanding helps create balanced relationships and healthier communities. (If I may push the men - "What was Adam doing while Eve was being deceived?")

Staying focused, this discussion is about parenting. When it comes to raising children, God's best is a two parent household. While one parent might demonstrate stronger leadership qualities, who bears the primary responsibility for guiding the family from a Biblical perspective? Consider the wisdom in 1 Corinthians 11:1, which offers this important principle, "Follow my example, as I follow the example of Christ."

If you notice that the men and women in your church aren't prioritizing their relationship with Christ above all else, including the spiritual leaders, consider finding a new congregation. While the seven churches in Revelation remind us that perfection doesn't exist, focus on finding a community that offers trust, accountability, dedicated service, and an environment where your children can flourish.

When do I let go?

When is the right moment to release someone you've watched grow from discovering insects, learning to ride a bike, mastering fishing, and developing speech, to becoming independent? It's undoubtedly difficult to watch someone you've nurtured embark on their own life journey. From a loving standpoint, this transition might consume much of your energy and time.

It's natural and necessary for children to develop independence from their parents. Genesis teaches us that a man should leave his parents and unite with his wife as one. This raises the question: What about those who aren't heading toward marriage? Remember, you still maintain a responsibility to support children. This is a part of being neighborly and builds a healthy worldview beyond your household.

Now that your child has moved forward, your role is to evaluate the effectiveness of you and your partner's parenting approach. Stay prepared to provide support while they continue developing their support system.

Understanding financial management and making sound monetary decisions remains a common struggle. This challenge exists regardless of wealth status. Many people, rich or poor, mismanage their resources and opportunities. If both you and your child's family need financial guidance, view it as an opportunity for collaborative learning.

Nevertheless, their new household with their spouse should be their primary focus. The Bible addresses this concept of caring for aging parents: "Very truly I tell you, when you were younger you dressed yourself and went where you wanted; but when you are old you will stretch out your hands, and someone else will dress you and lead you where you do not want to go" (John 21:18, NIV). Release control so their home becomes a sanctuary. Their home needs to be free from tension, resentment, worry, vengeance, or anger. Aim for an environment of love and security. You must model forgiveness, grace, and repentance because you may have to be led by your child some day.

Young children should begin preparing early for eventual independence. When possible, encourage them to seek employment and purchase appropriate clothing that aligns with your family values. This helps them understand conflict resolution before leaving home. While sports and clubs are beneficial, employment often presents unique challenges and conversations beyond typical group activities.

This approach might sound logical and could already align with your plans. Use employment as a way to assess your parenting effectiveness. Are you confident your child grasps financial concepts and conflict management? Many people describe their thirties and forties as recovery periods from their twenties' mistakes. Anyone with a proper worldview does not want their parenting hesitations to evolve into mental health issues or financial quandaries for their child.

You are letting go at a pace everyone involved can handle.

How do I communicate the unknown?

Communication barriers between family members are a natural part of the life cycle (from newborn to elderly). Don't view these challenges as failures. Remember that your child is experiencing everything for the first time. Practice patience. This is why we write in journals, pause before speaking, and pay attention to both spoken words and silent signals.

Building and keeping open communication with your growing child can be challenging. When they're of a different gender or enter their teenage years with judgmental attitudes, it often creates barriers. As the adult nurturing mentor, ensure you're not contributing to the problem. *The more mature person in any relationship bears the responsibility to heal it.* Sometimes, the other person might not be able to participate due to their own pain, stress, or lack of emotional maturity.

Young children typically hang on to your every word. As they grow older, this changes. This is when you need to adjust your expectations. Earlier, we discussed walking your child to school. Don't use this time to lecture them about rules or reminisce about your own childhood walks with your father. While these stories might open dialogue, let the child lead the conversation about whatever interests them. Ask thoughtful follow-up questions to understand if their words carry extreme consequences or just something they desire to say out loud. Bear in mind you are building trust.

Children face peer pressure and social challenges throughout their development stages. Supporting them in managing friendships, dealing with bullies, and developing self-confidence requires helping them formulate healthy thinking patterns. While listening, you might discover concerning behaviors, such as your child becoming a bully or is easily bullied. Avoid immediate judgment of yourself or your child. Listen carefully to understand their complete perspective. Be bold enough to consult with your spouse, your church community, and seek guidance through prayer before responding.

"Instead, speaking the truth in love, we will grow to become in every respect the mature body of Him who is the head, that is, Christ" (Ephesians 4:15, NIV). This aligns with 1 John 3:18 (ESV)'s teaching for parents: "Little children, let us not love in word or talk but in deed and in truth."

When the time comes to step back, you can feel confident knowing you've demonstrated strong principles, maintained open communication, and consistently pursued a healthy worldview. The challenge of dealing with children is overcome by the return on your investment in their lives.

Chapter 7

Survive, Alive, or Thrive

Each of us has two distinct modes of operating in life: the quick "go mode" where we act instantly, and the thoughtful "let me think about this mode" where we pause and reflect. Between these two extremes lies a balanced approach that can help us navigate life's challenges. The secret to living fully is to push ourselves just a little beyond our comfort zone, going that extra mile when we'd normally stop. When we consistently stretch ourselves this way, we discover that our progress accelerates beyond what we thought possible. We can go further faster. This creates a wonderful cycle. Our life begins to feel more meaningful and complete. We develop a deeper awareness of ourselves and our potential, which opens doors to new possibilities and fulfilling personal growth.

And to go further faster, you must recognize where you are in a particular area of your life. Patience moves you quicker than most believe.

Questions:
- What is survival mode?
- How to recognize being alive?
- What does it mean to thrive?

Have you noticed during group projects, whether in academics or professional settings, that team dynamics often reveal two distinct types: those who give minimal effort and those who fully commit? Do you ever pause to reflect on why certain teammates choose to do the bare minimum, failing to give their best to the project, the organization, or their own growth? People fall short of success for various reasons. A common barrier is their tendency to stay in their comfort zone, believing that achievement isn't meant for them.

What is survival mode?

Survival isn't just about enduring; it's a profound act of self-deception. When we're fighting to get by, we're often the ones fooling ourselves. We create narratives that aren't true, convict ourselves with faulty evidence, and contradict our own deepest beliefs just to make it through the day.

Many people only see what's right in front of them. Those stuck in survival mode often talk about personal development. Unfortunately, many remain trapped because they deceive themselves. Their aspirations and efforts lack staying power. They focus solely on quick wins or instant gratification. Quick wins often mean basic survival needs, as reflected in this wisdom: "Everyone's toil is for their mouth, yet their appetite is never satisfied" (Ecclesiastes 6:7NIV). Yes, we must eat to live; however, what about planning for the future? And instant gratification leads to poor choices, such as purchasing an unaffordable car with plans to return it within a couple of months.

The scripture says do not worry about tomorrow (Matthew 6:34). Breaking free from survival mode requires more than just living day-to-day—it demands a strategy. That strategy is building relationships.

⬅ **Survive, Alive, or Thrive** ➡

When we're stuck in survival thinking, our connections become purely transactional. Once we get what we need, we discard even those who helped us survive. It's like shopping at different stores. While we may be loyal to some places, with others, we simply fulfill our needs and move on.

When you're just trying to survive, the only thing that matters is right now. People who live this way don't expect much from life because they aren't sure they'll make it to tomorrow. This means any deal, transaction, or trade-off feels okay to them.

Now, not every single action in survival mode is this simple, but to grow we must first understand where we are. Many people think they're moving past their old struggles, but they end up repeating the same old mistakes. This is a common pattern.

Even when people in survival mode try to believe there's more to life, they often silently blame others for their problems or feel unworthy. Once you notice this in yourself, you have to ask a simple question: What is your responsibility?

Ponder this thought: When a stranger asks you, "Who are you?" does your response change based on your relationships with others? If those important people in your life never crossed your path, would you define yourself differently? Remember, your worth exists independently of others (or an organization).

Real growth demands expanding your vision beyond your immediate surroundings. Uncover your purpose and life goals independently, rather than letting others define who you are. Never allow another person's success or influence to hold you back from reaching your highest potential—especially when building a future that stretches beyond the next couple of days.

When you're just surviving, you often tie your identity to others to feel purposeful. Whether in your marriage or career, you might be progressing well. Yet, it's crucial to develop your individual strength. You are inherently complete and valuable (Colossians 2:6-10). This isn't about rejecting the bond with your partner. Instead, it's about bringing your unique qualities to strengthen the partnership.

Forcing a smile or masking your emotions with emptiness won't make things better. These are merely coping mechanisms that ultimately lead to nowhere. Many of us put on a happy face to convince others we're flourishing—as if we've got everything figured out. But when we pause to truly examine ourselves, we often realize we're not living authentically. That artificial happiness becomes our shield. For our emotional wellbeing and the sake of those who look up to us for guidance (our children or friends), we must learn to be genuine.

In Matthew 6:17-18, Jesus teaches, "But when you fast, anoint your head and wash your face, that your fasting may not be seen by others but by your Father who is in secret. And your Father who sees in secret will reward you." God sees through our facades and knows when we're just surviving.

What does "the pretend" (or putting on a show) really mean? We often seek sympathy or some form of validation from others during difficult times, falling into performance behavior. This represents survival mode in action—a fleeting and inauthentic connection. Survival mode drives us to form quick, transactional relationships before moving on. But, what we truly require is empathy in action. We need to gain clarity about our life circumstances and then take meaningful steps based on that understanding.

← **Survive, Alive, or Thrive** →

Many of us are in survival mode in at least one area of our lives. Life requires growth, yet we remain frozen, deceiving ourselves about our desire for change.

Staying stagnant isn't the answer. Finding joy solely in the present moment is fleeting—it doesn't eliminate anxiety about what's ahead. People overcome this anxiety by embracing the now while thoughtfully mapping their future. True living means recognizing that today's wise choices shape tomorrow's possibilities.

Colossians 1:23 (NIV) offers this, "We want each of you to show this same diligence to the very end, so that what you hope for may be fully realized." When we're just surviving, we operate transactionally because we lack hope's reassurance. Chapter 12 goes deeper into the concept of hope.

Let's look at what it really means to survive when you know you could be doing more.

This isn't for people who are barely getting by. This chapter is about the walls we build in our own minds. It's about being able to see the real purpose of our lives, and the lives of our families, clearly.

Think about it: If you went back to school while raising your kids, who would help you? Even the most supportive couples need help to achieve their goals.

Life is full of responsibilities: getting kids ready, going to work, preparing meals, and spending time with family. So, starting a business or changing careers takes a lot of time and sacrifice when paired with all those responsibilities. In survival mode, we often tell ourselves, "I'll do it one day." But instead of holding onto our plans, we need to give them to God. He made us and made a space for our future. All we have to do is ask with good intentions, and He will open doors.

← Challenging Your Worldview →

Just as Matthew 7:11 (NIV) reminds us, "If you, then, though you are evil, know how to give good gifts to your children, how much more will your Father in heaven give good gifts to those who ask him!"

Many people think that moving from survival to being alive is the same as winning. But this kind of "winning" can be misleading if we haven't practiced what we've learned from our past. It's also important to remember that some people don't want to get up at all. They will resent you for pushing them to be a winner.

How to recognize being alive?

Small victories are wonderful. String them together and we feel vibrant, alive, and accomplished. It is good. Celebration is a must. It is part of being alive.

Then comes the drive to tackle the next challenge. Perhaps your company has expanded to new territories and built a strong digital footprint. Maybe your family life is unfolding exactly as you envisioned. Or you've helped your niece graduate debt-free. These accomplishments make you feel fantastic. You may think, "I'm alive and winning!"

In these moments, life feels extraordinary. The opportunity to reach goals energizes us. You reflect, "My careful planning and dedication are paying off. People are recognizing it. My leisure time exceeds what my wife and I ever imagined possible." Yet we must acknowledge those around us whose similar efforts haven't yielded comparable results.

Given your leisure time status; do you think about the others around you? Be bold enough to ask if your business peers or co-worker's vacation consists of the same as yours. Do not pry; just listen and be curious. If you share similar positions, what creates the difference? Do you have a responsibility to share?

When you're in survival mode, you focus on the present moment. When you're in the alive mode, you reflect on your victories (Luke 12:18-21). Recognizing the alive mode means being open to learning and combining new knowledge with existing insights to create your next victory. This mindset stems from your commitment to maintain being alive.

What do you plan to do with this knowledge you gain? "A discerning person keeps wisdom in view, but a fool's eyes wander to the ends of the earth" (Proverbs 17:24 NIV). Seeking knowledge is valuable. Yet we must ask ourselves, "Am I gathering this information solely to fuel my personal accomplishments?"

Your actions and accomplishments aren't just random events. They're signposts guiding you toward a clear destination. Think of it like following a map to treasure. When we're truly alive and engaged, we don't just drift aimlessly. Instead, we take meaningful steps: creating solid plans, diving into books that expand our minds, signing up for classes to grow our skills, building relationships that matter, and putting in the hard work needed to see real results. As these efforts come to fruition, we begin to understand more about ourselves and what we believe we can achieve.

Sure, we all fall short of our intended outcomes. That's just part of being human. But how we handle those setbacks reveals whether we're truly living or merely surviving. When you're in this "alive mode," it's easy to get caught up in the excitement of your plans and goals. The energy feels invigorating! But there's wisdom in Psalm 37:4 (ESV) that reminds us: "Delight yourself in the Lord, and he will give you the desires of your heart." This teaches us something crucial. While being energized and motivated is wonderful, we need to be mindful of where we place our ultimate focus.

Remember to stay grateful for being alive, but also understand that this journey of being truly alive is leading you somewhere meaningful. Your destination matters longer than your journey—eternal life.

What does it mean to thrive?

A student sat beside his mentor watching a basketball game. The mentor posed a thoughtful question: "What do you think is the real purpose of church?" After brief contemplation, the student confidently answered, "It's a place where we go to receive what we need for ourselves. To ensure our own wellbeing."

In Colossians 1:28 (NIV) Apostle Paul writes, "He (The Messiah) is the one we proclaim, admonishing and teaching everyone with all wisdom, so that we may present everyone fully mature in Christ." This reveals a deeper truth about finding fulfillment and understanding a path to thrive.

People who are fully persuaded put their faith in action and other people who are just convinced see the world through what they believe. The empowering aspect comes from truly understanding how to thrive. Through our experiences, we develop trust and insight into how various situations will unfold or succeed. The optimistic worldview enables us to give freely, care authentically, and grow consistently. Faith helps us understand that even when people seem unresponsive, they can still recognize the truth (2 Corinthians 3:2-3,

Romans 2:15, Jeremiah 31:33). It is the reason to thrive and never give up. We are fully persuaded.

Indeed, we possess the power to reject reality before us. That is our freedom as a fallen people. Our judgment gets clouded by survival instincts from our past, shaped by misguided allegiances. Now, our goal is much greater as we mature. Growth becomes essential. Otherwise, we can't thrive.

To determine if you're thriving in life, focus on these essential elements:

1. Take time to reflect consistently. This could mean keeping a journal or connecting with a wise mentor who provides honest feedback about your worldview and whether it extends beyond self-focus. In other words, are you a walking contradiction to your own maturity, morals, and values?
2. After discovering what's genuine, reaffirm it through continuous learning. Engage in meaningful conversations and expand your knowledge through reading.
3. Transform your understanding into action. Confirmation is essential, and implementation helps deepen your comprehension (John 20:21).
4. Thriving involves considering the present, what lies ahead, and others' wellbeing. It means embracing your life lessons and applying them to benefit your community, the church, professional environment, those you guide, and family.

Thriving means knowing your current role and preparing for the next one. Of course, no one gets it perfect. But that's the beauty of discovery and living with grace. We must trust that our success depends on God's blessings. Never lean on your own understanding of a particular situation. It will likely take you back to a survival mode. Refresh the situation by taking a deep breath and praying. Then trust that your success relies on God's blessings.

So, where are you right now?

- *Are you stuck in survival mode, telling yourself that change will come "someday"? Your days consist of going through motions without a concrete strategy. Survival means talking about dreams and better tomorrows without taking real steps.*

- *Are you simply existing, sensing there's potential for more but making only small shifts? Your focus centers mainly on personal and (sometimes) household needs. Other aspects suffer because you're caught up in daily victories. Being alive means creating plans, feeling invigorated, and taking action.*

- *Or are you thriving—expanding your horizons while lifting others up? Thriving means steady progress, supporting others' growth, and elevating every aspect of life. In this stage, we're excelling across multiple areas and eager to pass on our wisdom. If you're hesitant to share, what holds you back? True prosperity extends beyond your immediate circle of family and friends.*

Truth is, we are all in different modes in the various aspects of our lives. While some areas of our existence flourish, others may remain stagnant. Getting sidetracked is a natural part of the journey. Keep in mind that success in one city doesn't guarantee the same even in a neighboring town. Some locations will celebrate your achievements, while others will reveal areas where growth is needed. Sometimes, reaching your full potential requires relocating to a different community, city, or region. Throughout history, countless individuals have relocated to create better opportunities for themselves.

So, how do you measure progress? Only God can give you the true answer. Proverbs 16:3 says, "Commit your works to the Lord and your plans will be achieved."

During moments of uncertainty, contradiction, or struggle, you can always reconnect with faith and thrive. It starts with listening and believing the Creator's truth over your own fears. That includes your professional path, spiritual life, relationships—and guiding others toward the same understanding.

Living isn't enough—we must thrive. This means embracing a lifestyle of sharing and helping others, aligned with your relationship with Christ. The Gospel of Jesus must be shared. A private follower of Christ isn't truly following at all (Acts 1:8, John 20:21, Psalm 96:3, Matthew 24:14, Mark 16:15, Romans 1:16, John 10:10).

Chapter 8

You Should Judge Me

Relationships between men and women evolve through distinct phases. Initial attraction, deepening connection, and lasting partnership. These stages unfold naturally as we grow together and understand each other, we judge each other. To judge simply means to make a decision regarding what life presents you. Transitioning from early romance to enduring love reveals the true nature of how you'll treat me (your main human investment) and everyone else.

Questions:
- What does it mean to judge correctly?
- After my verdict, what next?

An elderly woman rushes upstairs after hearing a concerning thud above. Her mind races to her beloved spouse of 45 years, anxiety building with each step. Just before reaching the top, her house slippers twist, sending her tumbling backward down the staircase.

Alone in the house with no visitors expected, her desperate pleas for assistance echo through empty rooms. Hours pass as she continues calling out. Understanding the severity of her situation, she eventually manages to drag herself to the telephone and contacts emergency services. The police arrive.

At the scene, a young officer documents the situation with photographs while his seasoned colleague surveys the area. After conferring, the veteran officer declares, "The evidence suggests she deliberately fell down the stairs following her husband's murder. Likely attempted murder-suicide gone awry." The perplexed junior officer inquires, "Take me through how you arrived at that conclusion?"

What does it mean to judge correctly?

Sharing life with someone special should create happiness, not resentment. Tranquility, not chaos. Connection, not obstacles. When you find yourself constantly saying sorry, it signals that these negative elements have grown overwhelming.

How can we reduce the need for constant apologies? The change begins within. A proper worldview involves showing kindness to yourself first. This means examining your own actions before critiquing those of others.

As flawed humans trying to collaborate with other imperfect individuals in church, educational institutions, families, or at work, we encounter challenges. Start by looking inward. Matthew 7:4 (NIV) highlights our approach: "How can you say to your brother, 'Let me take the speck out of your eye,' when all the time there is a plank in your own eye?" In simpler terms, you've overlooked your own obvious shortcomings and weaknesses while pointing out someone else's minor flaws.

Before passing judgment on others, pause and reflect: If I were in their shoes, what would I need? How would I want others to handle decisions that affect my life? The power of understanding cannot be understated.

While traditions and established protocols in families and workplaces have their place, don't let them be the sole guide. Yes, respect reputable guidelines. But take a moment to consider whether your decision will positively impact the person's future. This isn't about legal proceedings or crime victims. Rather, it's about supporting someone who's struggling to find their path or has made poor choices while dealing with life's challenges.

Consider this scenario: A team member consistently arrives late, facing potential termination. What's your perspective? Though they don't report to you directly, their actions reflect poorly on the team. Can you make a difference? Absolutely. Listen attentively to understand their challenges and offer guidance on better time management. Perhaps their background lacked structure or routine? Sometimes understanding someone's story can lead to meaningful solutions.

We all have blind spots where we need guidance. Romans 2:1 (ESV) reminds us wisely, "Therefore you have no excuse, O man, every one of you who judges. For in passing judgment on another you condemn yourself, because you, the judge, practice the very same things."

When we evaluate our spouse, family, or colleagues, we should do so with empathy and compassion, aiming to inspire positive change in their lives. Our purpose isn't to condemn. A Biblical worldview teaches us: "Nevertheless, when we are judged in this way by the Lord, we are being disciplined so that we will not be finally condemned with the world" (1 Corinthians 11:32). By following Christ's example, our actions and decisions should focus on supporting and directing others toward growth.

After my verdict, what next?

Follow up and follow through. You took the initiative to help your coworker with their punctuality, and now they arrive on time consistently. This positive change has created a ripple effect. Your team's performance and productivity have improved noticeably. But your role as a supportive colleague doesn't end here. You can still make a difference by boosting team morale. Even if you're naturally reserved, share small words of encouragement or simple observations that show you care. Remember, not every contribution needs to be dramatic or life-changing. Sometimes, the smallest gestures of support can create the most meaningful impact in your workplace relationships.

If you have culinary talents or financial means, consider bringing delicious homemade dishes to share with your colleagues. For those who are creative, use the breakroom as a gallery of achievements and recognition. These genuine gestures create meaningful connections and boost workplace morale. Remember, authentic celebration brings people together and builds community (Luke 15:31-32).

Now, those who have supported you in the past may someday need your assistance. Perhaps they'll ask for a ride to work or help with moving to a new home. And there might be times when you can't fulfill their requests as you would hope. Will you choose bitterness or retaliation? A wise person understands life's ebb and flow, keeping any disenchantment to themselves while focusing on gratitude for past kindnesses.

When you help others, it's important to remember that your judgment, assistance, and morale boosting shouldn't be driven by what you might get in return. A healthy and bold worldview comes from having a pure heart and genuinely wanting to make a difference in people's lives. Whenever you find yourself faced with a chance to help, take action without hesitation. Once you've done what you can, learn to let go and trust that you've made an impact. Our purpose is similar to a lighthouse. A guide to those who have lost their way. This reminds us of important teachings in Luke 5:32 and Romans 5:8, which tell us how Christ's love was so great that He actively sought out those who were struggling and transformed their lives through His ultimate sacrifice.

Making good judgments means identifying those who need basic support—whether it's guidance or just someone to listen to their struggles. Take a moment to reflect and ask yourself if you're the right person to help. If you feel you're not the best fit, there's no shame in directing them to someone better equipped—even if that person is a family member. Then following up with them to see how they're progressing. When possible, share examples from your own life that might inspire them, just as Matthew 5:14-16 teaches us to let our light shine before others.

This becomes especially important in our closest relationships with family and friends. These connections give us natural opportunities to practice compassion and understanding. Remember, every small act of kindness creates ripples of positive change in someone's life. By focusing on genuine help, we not only lift others up but also grow stronger in our own character and purpose.

Chapter 9

Power

Too often, our self reflection displays only what we have at our disposal. However, there are countless valuable tools and resources available to help us understand any situation more deeply. One of the most powerful tools we have access to is other people. They offer unique insights through conversations, shared experiences, and different forms of expression. The real power happens when we start to recognize what these interactions reveal about our own potential and limitations. During self-reflection, ask yourself: What power are others helping me discover outside of myself?

Questions:
- Does God's power work the way I want it to?
- Where do I look for power?

A young child watches his older brother racing ahead on the street. Eager to catch up, his sandal strap breaks unexpectedly, sending him on a tumble. His elder brother notices and immediately comes to help him off the pavement. Tears flowing, the little boy clings to his caring brother until they reach home. Their mother examines him and, despite his continued crying, offers a warm smile, gentle kiss, and bandage for his gently scraped knee. Comforted and relieved by the love, the little boy's tears fade as his spirit to play returns.

Does God's power work the way I want it to?

The previous paragraph displays a certain amount of authority and power. Three individuals who demonstrate unique forms of power. The young lad radiates the ability to spark joy and affection, while his older brother embodies security and guardianship. The mother figure represents nurturing energy and restorative grace.

These qualities mirror only a part of the divine nature of our Creator, who thoughtfully distributes these gifts among humanity. This distribution creates our fundamental need for connection and community. When we unite our individual strengths, we unlock potential far greater than we often recognize. As written in 1 Corinthians 12:15 (ESV), "If the foot should say, 'Because I am not a hand, I do not belong to the body,' that would not make it any less a part of the body." You remain an essential piece of both your church and local community. Your active participation matters deeply, as others depend on your unique contribution to not only advance our shared mission but to sustain our collective power through unified purpose.

← Power →

In Genesis 11, we discover the remarkable potential of those who constructed the Tower of Babel. While these earthly beings could never match the Creator's magnificence, they risked stepping beyond divine guidance and protection. By doing so, they likely abandoned their true source of power and authority. When humanity strayed from God's intended path and purpose, divine intervention became necessary to thwart their erroneous power. Consider this: Did those people in the Land of Shinar truly understand the risks of their ambitious venture, like the thinning air at great heights?

God's power manifests through protecting and nurturing us, not through imposing restrictions or distance. True love exists in its purest form through God alone, flowing eternally and unconditionally.

We might strive to find power within ourselves; yet, we should remember the powerful words from 2 Corinthians 1:21-22 (NIV): "Now it is God who makes both us and you stand firm in Christ. He anointed us, set his seal of ownership on us, and put His Spirit in our hearts as a deposit, guaranteeing what is to come." Only through God's power are your former behaviors nullified. No amount of personal introspection can match the life-changing power of God's salvation. Discovering your authentic self and personal growth comes through surrendering to your divine Creator's loving guidance. Run away from creating yourself as an idol. Then the question becomes: What do you run towards? Christ gives you purpose and definition (1 Peter 2:9-10).

Where do I look for power?

Where are you on your path to self-discovery? When you recognize that finding salvation is essential to truly understanding yourself, you've already begun your transformative journey toward accepting your place in God's divine plan and spiritual family.

The unmatched power of Jesus Christ manifests itself in ways we often don't immediately recognize, like in the young boy's story at the start of this chapter. As Psalm 119:7 reminds us: "It was good that I was afflicted, that I might learn your statutes." The mother's nurturing actions demonstrate how healing and solace can emerge from difficult situations, much like Jesus showed through his continuous stream of miraculous works.

Divine intervention appears everywhere around us. For example, home construction for those in need, food banks serving the hungry, and in medical services. This naturally leads us to ponder: Why doesn't God simply eliminate all suffering and need?

Let's consider what James writes in chapter two. He asks what good is it if you have faith in God and you do not use the simple powers bestowed upon you. Those powers means providing food, clothing, and shelter to others. It is a simple way to honor what God presents to you (a reciprocal relationship). Some of us have far more than we will ever need and we do share. And many with a lot less also share. That is the power of God working through all of us (2 Corinthians 6:1). Faith is a relationship of power with the Creator that you are okay and will be okay. The power belongs to God and was turned over to us to use in connection with God.

What about those who've struggled for years? The Creator's grand design includes the gift of eternal life as part of this empowerment. Your actions reveal your faith more than empty words ever could (James 2:18). Whether you can only manage worship and prayer due to your *extreme* circumstances, the Creator sees and values

⬅ **Power** ➡

your faith (Hebrews 11:6). Connect with others, step forward confidently, and spread this message. Remember, we're all working alongside God in this journey (1 Corinthians 3:9).

Chapter 10

Mom, the Unicorn Is Acting Weird

Have you experienced an instinct or dream that felt so real that you had to document it? Did it manifest into reality (or something remarkably close)? Did you pause to consider its significance? Could it be a sign the spirit realm is reaching out with a message meant only for you? Some might say, "This experience was meant to prepare you." Remember, this is a message only you have witnessed.

Questions:
- Have you gazed into the depths of the ocean and questioned what other wonders remain unseen?
- Who experiences the supernatural world?
- How do we embrace science?

Reaching this part of the book means you already get that a healthy worldview leads you to God, the unseen (Romans 1:20). The Bible's teachings and God's qualities help explain how God works as a Creator and a Relational Being. A Spirit who loves you so much that there's always a way to have a relationship with your Creator, but you're still free to make that choice.

Have you gazed into the depths of the ocean and questioned what other wonders remain unseen?

In the depths of our consciousness, where imagination meets faith, we often struggle to embrace the spiritual dimensions of our faith journey. Many find it challenging to accept the concept that God exists as a spiritual being.

Watch young children as they explore the outdoors. Their eyes light up at every butterfly, tiny insect or undiscovered plant. Their pure wonder reminds us of God's infinite creative power at work. When we ponder why such diverse creatures exist, we can find answers in Revelation's description of various beings surrounding God's throne (Revelation 4:6-8).

Just as heaven holds this diversity, earth mirrors it wondrously. The vast oceans teem with countless species, leading some to embrace evolutionary theory. Whether these beings evolved matters less than understanding what set this magnificent process in motion. If you believe a tadpole transformed into a whale over time, what divine force orchestrated this remarkable journey of transformation? (Evolution is not in line with scriptural teachings Genesis 1:20-27.)

The Creator applies boundless knowledge to establish perfect conditions for every planet and its life forms. God masterfully designed each planet's contents and ensured all creatures can adapt, by His will, through expected transformations.

In the heavenly realm (or spiritual domain), this principle holds true. The ability to appear in God's presence and navigate the spiritual landscape is essential, as shown in Revelation 4. The elders and beings did not just sit; they moved.

When God designed life forms for Earth, inspiration came from the spirit realm's existing beings. In Revelation 4, we encounter descriptions of magnificent creatures—some resembling oxen, another with a human face, and some like eagles. This divine connection helps us understand why, as we study Scripture and deepen our relationship with God, we find both familiar elements and awe-inspiring creativity.

Next time you stand before a vast ocean stretching endlessly into the distance, ponder the incredible diversity of marine life below—from the tiniest microorganisms that escape our eyes to the grand creatures that leave us yearning for a closer encounter.

Who experiences the supernatural world?

The inspiring truth is everyone does—whether you're navigating marriage, battling illness, facing solitude, pursuing your dreams, or, like that brave single dad, raising two precious daughters. Remember, we all share the gift of life's breath from God (Genesis 2:7).

Our deepest power lies in the divine spark that resides within us as earth's chosen beings. Through this sacred connection, we possess the remarkable ability to communicate with God about anything, anytime we choose. As 1 John (ESV) reminds us, "And this is the confidence that we have toward Him, that if we ask anything according to His will He hears us." When we let go of societal norms, ingrained habits, and ego-driven desires (idol worship), we rediscover our innate spiritual potential.

After His resurrection, Jesus gives instructions about what's going to happen next. In the book of John, Jesus talks about a spiritual force who will be with humanity forever. To show that God the Father, the Son (Jesus the Anointed One), and the Holy Spirit are all in agreement as the same being, Jesus says, "I will ask the Father, and He will give you another Advocate (or Helper) who will never leave you" (John 14:16).

It is not about the clear signal to your spiritual connection like a cell tower; it is about the faith and willingness to be in relationship with God the Father. Romans 8:26 (ESV), "Likewise the Spirit helps us in our weakness. For we do not know what to pray for as we ought, but the Spirit himself intercedes for us with groanings too deep for words." Have you ever thought of those who cannot do works as expressions of their faith or who can't speak clearly to pray? God has already planned for their success in faith.

Romans 8:27 (NIV) teaches, "And He who searches our hearts knows the mind of the Spirit, because the Spirit intercedes for God's people in accordance with the will of God." He guides us on a journey as fit for the good things of God. We share with others the transformative peace we discover in relationship with God. Many struggle to comprehend their spiritual awakening, feeling unsettled as it challenges their familiar beliefs and culture.

Throughout our diverse world, countless belief systems and cultural perspectives make it challenging to grasp fully spiritual manifestations and wonders. In Acts 2, we read of people misinterpreting spiritual phenomena as intoxication simply because it's unfamiliar to them. When the Apostle Peter speaks up, he illuminates the powerful workings of the Spirit—from prophetic dreams to divine visions and beyond. It's natural to question things we haven't personally witnessed or experienced. This highlights why continuous learning and personal growth through study become essential for our spiritual journey.

It is important to say that a family should be a solid unit. And life presents opportunities for families and friends to interact with those holding diverse beliefs and perspectives. Your role is to shield your family while navigating spiritual quests. Always remember that your primary connection is with God—the only relationship that truly lasts forever. When questioned about a woman who married multiple brothers sequentially (following tradition), Jesus provided this profound insight: "Jesus replied, 'You are in error because you do not know the Scriptures or the power of God'" (Matthew 22:29 NIV). In God's infinite power, we find complete fulfillment, requiring nothing else.

This brings us to the matter of seeking spiritual guidance through mediums, crystals, and necromancy. Why would anyone need an intermediary to connect with the spiritual realm when we have an intercessor in Christ and the Holy Spirit as our advocate (Romans 8:34, Hebrews 4:15-16, John 14:26)? Our understanding of supernatural experiences should always be filtered through the lens of Christ's redemptive work in our lives. The scripture in Leviticus 19:31

(ESV) provides clear guidance: "Do not turn to mediums or necromancers; do not seek them out, and so make yourselves unclean by them: I am the Lord your God." This emphasizes our responsibility to maintain a pure spiritual connection.

Ponder this: One path leads to a being whose title is deceiver, destroyer, and dragon (Revelation 12:9)? The other path leads to the ultimate Healer, Comforter, Counselor, Helper, Savior, Mighty King, and Messiah. So what's your choice? For many, the choice depends on their spiritual perspective and worldview. Ask yourself: Since I will experience the supernatural, does it serve my highest good to embrace beliefs that contradict my proclaimed morals and values?

How do we embrace science?

Think about something fascinating—how delicate is the balance of life and the being who orchestrates it all. If God can design digestive acids strong enough to break down food in our stomach, surely that same Creator can create a protective barrier to withstand that same acid—our stomach lining. Have you considered this perspective? Every aspect of creation serves a purpose, including the spiritual realm.

You are probably aware that many people today attempt to detect spiritual presence through various technological means. Ghost hunters commonly employ tools like EMF detectors, heat-sensing cameras, and sound recording devices to confirm supernatural presence. They believe that unexplained cold spots can indicate spirit activity, based on our understanding of normal heat patterns in the atmosphere and the energy field surrounding the human body. When an area that should maintain a consistent temperature shows an unexplained cold void, some interpret this as evidence of spiritual presence. While this offers a basic explanation, remember that all spiritual beings, like angels, must serve a purpose.

Angels and spirits primarily function as divine messengers. Unfortunately, not all spiritual entities bring positive messages. Some do not come in peace and seek to separate us from God our Father. As the Bible teaches us, angels can manifest in various forms: as human beings, through dreams, or in visions (referenced in Hebrews 1:14, Luke 1:11, Hebrews 13:2). When operating in service to God, angels help remind humanity of God's active presence in our lives.

The spiritual truth is beautifully captured in this passage: "This is how you can recognize the Spirit of God: Every spirit that acknowledges that Jesus Christ has come in the flesh is from God, but every spirit that does not acknowledge Jesus is not from God. This is the spirit of the antichrist, which you have heard is coming and even now is already in the world" (1 John 4:2-3, NIV).

In essence, any good spirit must recognize Jesus Christ is the embodiment of God and our Redeemer (Colossians 2:9). When encountering a spirit, be bold enough to question it thoroughly until you gain clarity. And if you've never been aware of such spiritual encounters, that's perfectly fine. Your personal journey toward salvation doesn't require matching someone else's exact experiences.

The Bible reveals that we will one day judge angels (1 Corinthians 6:3). These divine messengers who serve us will face judgment. This isn't about debating our worthiness or methods. Rather, it's about understanding science and the hierarchy of your present existence. As you move through life, you may question if your actions truly make a difference. They do.

This may cause you to consider the people who seem drawn to others who have lived in different times or have different cultural or spiritual beliefs. Take a stand and be bold in your worldview so that you can expand your knowledge while still holding fast to your own beliefs. As you read books, attend seminars, and watch videos about spirits (or ghosts), rest in the fact that they are real and are here to draw you closer to God the Father (or reveal the wickedness of the spirit realm which is another reason to draw closer to God).

The sound that goes bump in the night may just be the floor settling as an air bubble works its way into the house over time with rain and wind. Do not be afraid, and question any presence you encounter, whether in physical or spiritual form. It is your right to do so. Time and again in the Bible, you see angels telling those who receive a message, "Do not be afraid" (Luke 2:9-10, Matthew 1:20-21, Acts 27:23-25). Be bold enough to familiarize your children with the spiritual realm, the unknown, and different kinds of animals, including the one mentioned in the book of Job: Leviathan. This practice expands their culture and supports their scientific studies, making it easier to grow closer to an unseen deity (Colossians 1:15).

Chapter 11

You Need There to Be A God

You might be surprised by that bold title. It needs context. First, you have to understand that it's okay to *tolerate* people with different beliefs. To live in peace, however, you must be willing to question your own understanding of God. Second, this chapter won't discuss an atheistic point of view ad nauseam. Instead, it will explore how people with a greater understanding of the world can help others heal and grow as they learn about God.

Questions:
- What makes God worthy of worship?
- Is there a counsel of Gods?
- Is it proper to place my hope in God?
- How do the principles of God govern my worklife?

To set time, space, and matter into motion without limits, a being would have to exist outside of them. For example, when creating a painting, the artist must choose a canvas, a color palette, and brushes. Next, the painter must decide what to paint and how to achieve their perfect craft, as well as where to display it. The painter is not their work of art; it is an example of the artist's vision and some of their abilities.

What makes God worthy of worship?

Simple answer. God exists outside of the time space continuum.

The purposeful structure of DNA (Deoxyribonucleic Acid) reveals itself when we examine the intricate design. This remarkable molecular blueprint carries the essential code that maintains every living being throughout its life span, plus provides familial similitude. The precision of its design, coupled with its ability to adapt to environmental influences is amazing in and of itself. God's thoughtful creation is limitless. "Generations come and generations go, but the earth remains forever" as the Bible states in Ecclesiastes 1:4 (NIV).

When we observe the world around us and each other, it's fascinating to realize that despite our unique genetic codes (DNA), we share remarkably similar features: 2 eyes, a nose, 2 ears, and a mouth. And at the time of writing this book, our planet hosts billions of individuals, each distinctly different yet fundamentally alike.

This profound mystery deserves our deepest contemplation, analysis, and understanding—each answer leading to new questions; and more answers. The subject is far too significant to ever rest. Through sincere seeking, you begin to grasp the magnificence of God, even as just a concept. Even with eternal life, you'd never exhaust all there is to discover.

In his writings, Apostle Paul describes his revelation of Christ, considering everything else garbage or dung (Philippians 3:8, NIV and KJV). He recognizes that nothing—not even human relationships—compares to knowing Christ. This divine connection purifies us from worldly experiences and actions, demonstrating God's boundless love for humanity.

Referred to as the "Uncaused, First Cause", or God, He defines a relationship with humanity through His will. As a sovereign being without a beginning or end (Uncaused, First Cause), God operates within defined relationship parameters. Every insight and revelation you gain stems from your personal connection with the Creator.

A popular philosophical question asks, "Can God create a rock too heavy for Him to lift?" This query presupposes that God operates without relational limits. In truth, we partner with God as joint heirs with Christ. Therefore, such questions about divine power must be viewed through the lens of our collaborative relationship with God and His creation.

Did the Creator ever say He wouldn't lie? Yes, He did. Numbers 23:19 tells us that God is not a human who lies or changes His mind. This verse highlights the difference between God's unchanging character and the human tendency to be deceitful. God's promises are true—what God says, God does.

This brings us back to the question about the rock. If the Creator were to say a rock wouldn't be moved by God's power, then it would never be moved. The size of the rock doesn't matter. The real point of the question is not about power, but about our relationship with God and His truthfulness.

Honestly, we do not know everything about God. We must remember that in the book of Revelation 10:4, John writes about his experience. A voice instructed him not to write down what he witnessed. Think about the sun, for example. Though we may understand the science of how it creates energy, that doesn't fully explain the mystery of the different heat signatures. The real key to understanding comes from our relationship with our Creator. Our relationship provides us with understanding; without it, we are unable to truly grasp the depths of our world. That is why others without a relationship to any spiritual force have a resistance to such conversations.

God's ability to connect with any person, help them, heal them, offer an opportunity to change, and remain unseen (or be seen through the works of people in Christ) is remarkable. Because of this, the relationship with such a sovereign being makes God worthy of worship. If you accept that idea, be bold enough to maintain your fervor for serving the Lord (Romans 12:11).

Is there a counsel of Gods?

What is a person really saying when they mention all religions are the same or valid? Are they saying that any one god is the same as another god? Is that their point? To acknowledge other gods with the same footing means they share the same planet.

Does this suggest they hold equal status with other deities sharing our Earth (or multiverse)? However, for this exploration, let's concentrate solely on Earth.

You might hear different groups of people—like governments, cultures, or religious factions—talk about their god or beliefs. They often speak as if their god(s) are more important than everyone else's. This is not something to be admired, believed, or emphasized. These groups are not likely to claim mythology concerning what they believe. Remember, every group thinks their stories are true, but that doesn't make them facts.

Here are a few points of clarity using the Bible.

1. Any god that is not the God of the Bible is false. Even though Jesus calls people "god', He is not saying their ability and sovereignty are equal to the God -

    a. *"For great is the Lord and most worthy of praise; He is to be feared above all gods. For all the gods of the nations are idols, but the Lord made the heavens."* Psalm 96:4-5 (NIV)

    b. *"Jesus answered them, 'Is it not written in your Law, 'I have said you are 'gods.'"* John 10:34 (NIV)

2. "Let us make man in our image." This is also known as the "imago dei." The Christ, the Holy Spirit, and God are all one. God has given some of the qualities to people. These qualities include wise advice, creativity, harmony, authority, a feeling of longing, and love, among others.

    a. *"The Son is the image of the invisible God, the firstborn over all creation. For in him all things were created: things in heaven and on earth, visible and invisible, whether thrones or powers or rulers or authorities; all things have been created through him and for him. He* is before all things, and in him all things hold together." Colossians 1: 15-17 (NIV).

    b. "And I will pray the Father, and he shall give you another Comforter, that he may abide with you forever." John 14:16 (KJV)

3. The God of the Bible notes that it is detestable what people are doing to bolster other gods.

    a. "Then he brought me to the entrance of the north gate of the house of the Lord, and I saw women sitting there, mourning the god Tammuz. He said to me, 'Do you see this, son of man? You will see things that are even more detestable than this.'" Ezekiel 8:14-15 (NIV).

    b. He then brought me into the inner court of the house of the Lord, and there at the entrance to the temple, between the portico and the altar, were about twenty-five men. With their backs toward the temple of the Lord and their faces toward the east, they were bowing down to the sun in the east" Ezekiel 8:16 (NIV)

If all gods are the same, then why does one of those 'gods,' the God of the Bible, have a commandment in the Old Testament that says, "You shall have no other gods before me?" (Exodus 20:3 ESV). This statement is very powerful because it is an absolute command.

Is this a trivial matter to you? This idea is also supported in the New Testament when Jesus commands, "Love the Lord your God with all your heart and with all your soul and with all your mind"(Matthew 22:37 NIV). If there were many gods with the same power, one of them couldn't make this kind of claim over a planet they share with others. Don't you think this is a problem, given the power a supreme being is supposed to have?

It is imperative that you conclude the matter at hand. And as you do, the discussion must consider this passage from Psalm 97:9 (NIV), "For you, Lord, are the Most High over all the earth; you are exalted far above all gods." In order to further the premise of a "counsel of gods"- meaning gods that share the same planet and are different versions of the same god - you either have to exclude the God of the Bible or accept the premise is flawed.

Is it proper to place my hope in God?

We're hoping that our friends come and get us, or a rideshare driver gets us to our destination on time. Does this sound like you? It's nice to have hope in humanity. But, did you ever think about what makes your friends act? Love can and connection does. Those ideas come from God. 1 John 4:16 (NIV) states, "And so we know and rely on the love God has for us. God is love. Whoever lives in love lives in God, and God in them."

Does the love or connection of family remain? The connection is sustainable only as long as their ability and desire are sufficient to meet your needs. When they don't, it ends. Time, pain, disappointment, and consequence are disrupters to connection. Harsh as that sounds, you still have the Father to rely upon for what may be next in life's journey. The Good News in a nutshell. The only requirement is that you believe—have faith and act upon what you understand. You will continually discover more, that's what learning and increasing your faith is all about.

Share what you learn so that others may experience what you know. Then they, in turn, can use it, share it, and pass it along. What's more, they may discover something for you. In Hebrews 5, when speaking about Jesus as a High Priest, it's explained that many stop trying to understand. They need basic teaching repeated; instead of elevating their understanding, they are no longer willing to learn.

The problem with hope without Christ is that others are relying on you. When you say, "I'm hoping and praying," others may be in dire need of something to come from that hope. Empty words are temporary and may make either ourselves or someone else feel good, but to what end? We are still in need of water, food, clothing, and shelter.

What good are words when I am freezing if there isn't an assurance of an answer. Hebrews further explains, "Because God wanted to make the unchanging nature of His purpose very clear to the heirs of what was promised, he confirmed it with an oath" (Hebrews 6:17, (NIV). An oath we count on as we hope. A healthy worldview believes that each fleeting and brief moment is also precious and does work out for the best. Otherwise, your time spent alive here on earth is not just meaningless. It is meaningless to an end. This is why anyone who professes a modicum of understanding and a relationship with Jesus the Savior should be ready to give a reason for the hope you have in Christ. Offering a simple phrase a person may say the following:

Too often I make mistakes and do not live up to my promise. I believe in the deity and nature of a loving God; and, I desire a relationship. So can you. I do not have hope for hope's sake. My hope for a better tomorrow is placed in the One who can orchestrate it (Colossians 1:23, Hebrews 6:16-20).

How do the principles of God govern my worklife?

Discussing a relationship's tough answers means eventually getting to who and/or what God is. As discussed above, God is certainly a supreme being whose abilities and personal attributes make the Creator worthy of worship. Furthermore, God solves problems before they arise. In the first book of this series, relationships are discussed in more detail. In this volume, the chapter entitled "Marriage: Tying Down the Nuts and Bolts" has more information about husband and wife relationships.

These principles have been documented through various teachings and through exercises of those seeking a better way. Be bold enough to apply each of them so that your relationships flourish.

One of the first principles deals with colleagues. It's easy if they have the same general principles that govern their lives: Peace, harmony, teamwork, and seeking wisdom. The challenge comes from team members who insist on being contrarians or endless disruptors. You cannot abandon your core work. Beyond anything else, you are a follower of Christ, and that goes before any career choice.

In understanding that, remember, "But to you who are listening I say: Love your enemies, do good to those who hate you" (Luke 6:27, NIV). That's a challenge for any of us, especially when things escalate, as we want to protect ourselves. Unfortunately, you may be drawn in by colleagues. Stay vigilant and watch carefully so that you are not. Usually, a person who intends harm will reveal it if you pay close attention.

Another principle to guide relationships is by giving to a person who steals from you (Luke 6:30, Matthew 5:40).

Now is the part of the book where you should pause, take a breath, and remember God is in charge.

If Jesus provides these instructions to you as a person who submits to God, it is good. Allow them to have their fill, and remember Job 1:21. A worldview that is mature and wise expects people to be less than honorable. As unfortunate as it is, it is true.

Yes, I'm in agreement with you that there are some things you are not willing to let go of. The struggle is far beyond what another can imagine for a family heirloom or for lunch if you are barely able to pay for it. It is about perfecting your faith. An heirloom may have insurance. While not the same, it solves the issue. If you have your community, church, family, and friends, lunch will be possible. If you are using the other principles of character, most assuredly lunch will be provided. Because, when friendship and kindness depends on you, many things are possible.

In chapter 6 Luke recalls Jesus discussing the principles of hearing instructions but not using them for building a house, and "when a strong stream came the house was washed away completely" (paraphrase). A strong connection to a colleague is built on a healthy worldview of your character.

A last point to emphasize: You may never experience the outcome of the principles you display toward others. Point your colleagues and others you encounter toward Christ by how you conduct yourself. Do not just honor Christ with lip service. Be a peacemaker, forgive, and be helpful. But don't be helpful to the detriment of your job and health. But colleagues should greet you with peace when you arrive. If they do not, is your character or theirs the issue? Be bold enough to ask the tough questions and seek guidance (James 1:5).

Chapter 12
Truth: The Harsh Lesson

Did you know that truth is singular? When you take the stand in a court of law in the United States you are asked a question: '*Do you swear to tell the whole truths?*' Sounds wrong doesn't it?

We have to be careful because the truth we face can crush our culture, traditions, and beliefs. And that is a harsh lesson. The best worldview is the remarkable solution we all can share, that is—the truth stands firm.

Questions:
- When you lie, what do you gain?
- Why are there so many combative inhabitants?
- Can we break apart the truth and reconstruct it?

← Challenging Your Worldview →

A man in a suit walks into a courtroom and heads directly for the witness stand. He sits, crosses his legs, and looks directly at the judge. He notices the judge isn't making eye contact with anyone in particular, which sets him off. "Where is the bailiff!" the man yells. The judge looks at him and says, "We just want you to tell your story. There's no need for a bailiff to swear you in. You get it—everyone here is on the honor system." Now, if you had a choice, would you go back to that courtroom?

When You Lie What Do You Gain?

Lying about a particular situation may immediately provide a feeling of relief or protection.

So, let's examine the liar. The Bible, in John 8:44 (NIV), clarifies that we are not all God's children: "You belong to your father, the devil...When he lies, he speaks his native language, for he is a liar and the father of lies." You have a choice in what you say and how you deceive. While challenging when faced with a culture or tradition that rewards lying, it's essential that you seek a different path.

God's purpose is adoption. Our lives offer the chance to start anew when presented with new choices—like adoption into God's family. A key question to ask is: Why remain in a place where you're aware of constant deceit? Are the money, friendships, or career trajectory truly that enticing? Are you pursuing short-term gains, assuming no one will ever know? Most people believe they are honest. If that is a fair assessment, then abandoning old ways is a must if you want to be part of the solution to deception. To practice something different as part of the adopted family of God, speak slower, listen carefully, and be factual.

Indeed, no one is perfectly free of deceit. The Bible teaches us why we need salvation. However, your convictions should mature beyond what is now—clear and present. You may feel the need to protect yourself with deceit, as some might argue Rahab did in the book of Joshua, justifying the act. Is your lie, not Rahab's, about elevating your faith? Are you clear about it with God? Are you ready to stand before judgment as you utter words of deceit? Be bold enough to make a decision and pray during life's challenges. Remember, every action toward you doesn't have to be met with an expected reaction or practice.

1 John 3:8 (NIV) reminds us, "The one who does what is sinful is of the devil, because the devil has been sinning from the beginning. The reason the Son of God appeared was to destroy the devil's work." Be bold enough, through your faith in God, to join in this effort.

Why are there so many combative inhabitants?

People have a choice. They're innately programmed with a sense of right and wrong, and the book of Hebrews states that we have the law written on our hearts and minds (Hebrews 10:16). It's within us to know what to do: Choose yes or no, right or wrong, and decide whether to tell the truth or practice deceit.

How did this go astray within the Church? Even among believers, people have a choice between good and evil behaviors. A loving God provides a path to reconciliation. There are two main reasons this can go wrong.

First, not everyone in the church is aware of all the resources it offers, so they don't participate. Too many don't accept the relevance of what they know or the responsibility to get involved.

Second, consider Hebrews 10:29 (NIV): "How much more severely do you think someone deserves to be punished who has trampled the Son of God underfoot, who has treated as an unholy thing the blood of the covenant that sanctified them, and who has insulted the Spirit of grace?"

A combative inhabitant in the church who is ordained by God should be removed by fellow believers. The Bible says to break ties with those who are sexually immoral, greedy, idolaters, slanderers, drunkards, or swindlers. If a person continually practices these behaviors without repentance or seeking help, they aren't pursuing righteousness and truth. Offer them the peace of Christ and a chance to be won over—not by you, but by the power of Christ. Be bold enough to stand with them and guide them in the right direction. If you are that person, do the same. Grace and forgiveness come first, but then ties should be broken if they don't change.

Remember that working out your salvation isn't a one-day task. If the Most High asks you to isolate yourself, isn't it reasonable to ask why? Being on the path of righteousness and sharing the same planet with others sometimes requires solidarity to make sense of your experiences, unless your goal is to be a combative inhabitant. Moreover, isolating yourself from others seems counterintuitive to survival, given how much we need one another. Isolate to understand, and then share the truth you discover. As Psalm 25:5 (ESV) says, "Guide me in your truth and teach me, for you are God my Savior, and my hope is in you all day long."

← Truth: The Harsh Lesson →

Can we break apart the truth and reconstruct it?

The characteristics of truth can be broken down into rigidity, shareability, coherence, responsibility, and being recompensable.

1. **Rigidity of Truth**

Truth can seem pliable, but it's not. In a court of law, a verdict for the same act might appear to be different depending on the situation. However, the court structure takes all factors into account. The truth of what happened remains unchanged, regardless of how the hearers interpret it. There's a standard, and if the accused didn't follow it, there are consequences. Similarly, the Bible is clear about the consequences for those who do not follow its commands.

2. **Coherence and Reliability**

Have you ever heard someone at work or school say something that "doesn't add up?" Truth must be consistent and logical. When you test the truth, it always checks out. The actual conclusion doesn't change, even if you stop before you've finished testing it. When something is the truth, it is unchangeable. When something is true, it can change—for example, a stove is hot until it cools down.

Jesus brought a coherent message to those He taught. Paul acknowledged this in 1 Timothy 4:6 (ESV), saying, "If you put these things before the brothers, you will be a good servant of Christ Jesus, being trained in the words of the faith and of the good doctrine that you have followed." He then warned them, "Have nothing to do with irreverent, silly myths. Rather train yourself for godliness" (1 Timothy

4:7, ESV). The beauty of the reliability of truth is that we can always return to it.

3. Responsibility and Accountability

We must be responsible with the truth because it can lead people astray. As stated in 2 Timothy 2:15 (ESV), "Do your best to present yourself to God as one approved, a worker who has no need to be ashamed, rightly handling the word of truth." A solid worldview means you will stop an action you see that is disrupting the truth. Being bold with the truth even means stopping yourself.

Jesus laid down His life as a ransom for many. Is your life worth anything? Could it be bought? Jesus paid the price for those who choose to follow and for those who do not (John 3:16). You don't have to agree with God or the Bible to recognize the significance of this act. Any person, in any historical writing, willing to give their life for all people who exist or ever will exist, is almost incomprehensible.

A statement from such a person is just a statement until they follow through. Through His actions, God offered the life of Jesus for us, even though we were unworthy. You were made worthy because of love. That is a rigid, shareable, coherent, responsible, and recompensable truth from God that no other worldview can topple.

A CLOSING REQUEST

Will you do me a favor and treat your family better than they deserve? And, when you pray, add me to your list, and ask the Holy Spirit to guide you out of your dark days with the lesson intact.

"May you love well and live outrageously for Christ."
—Marcus L. Davis

Topics in Future Volumes

1. Winning Takes Place First
2. Cold-Hearted
3. Validity of Your Feelings
4. Like Vs. Love
5. A Heavy Healing Hand
6. The Purpose of Your Pastor
7. Relational Prayer
8. Follow

Author's Comments:

I am deeply grateful for your support—for those who have listened to my music, read my books, and sought my wise counsel. My greatest gift to you is the inspiration to live a better life in Christ.

As I shared in the first book of this series, I grew up attending a church in North Carolina, which sparked my curiosity about God. However, I didn't truly learn about faith, Jesus, or the foundations of the Bible until I was an adult. This personal history informs my work. Therefore, I enjoy speaking with someone who doesn't grasp these fundamentals discussed in this book. It can be challenging. My approach is to revisit the basics, offering advice from a consistent Biblical perspective until the concepts are understood.

My time is spent with friends, family, and others who are either unfamiliar with or do not accept Biblical principles, as well as with many fellow believers. Character is what keeps these relationships strong. While my non-believing friends may not always be receptive, I remain steady on my faith journey. Other books on my website draw on these relationships, using composite characters and ideas to bolster true connection. I am always hopeful and ready for anyone who wants to learn more.

The work I do—helping veterans, improving marriages, and coaching healthcare workers and business leaders—continues through my life coaching services. The purpose of my business and my discussions on different platforms is the same: To bring awareness to those in need of affordable housing and food. This mission drives the business model and donation structure of Marcus1Media, LLC, where a minimum of 50% of all net year-end profits is donated to this cause.

Thank you!

Scripture References by Chapter

1. **Strictly Business – When It's Personal**
   a. 2 Thessalonians 3:6
   b. Romans 16:17
   c. James 3:18 (NIV)
   d. Romans 12
   e. 1 Samuel 25
   f. James 4:14

2. **My Tomato, Your Tomato, Our Tomatoes**
   a. Luke 10:19
   b. 2 Timothy 1:7
   c. Isaiah 1:17
   d. Acts 4:34
   e. Micah 2:1-2
   f. Proverbs 28:3
   g. Matthew 22:39
   h. Mark 12:31

3. **Not My Friend**
   a. Luke 11:5-7
   b. Proverbs 22:24
   c. Proverbs 12:26

d. Proverbs 18:13
e. Psalm 109:4
f. Philippians 1:3-6
g. James 4:4
h. John 15:15
i. Mark 12
j. John 15:23

4. **Marriage – Tying Down the Nuts and Bolts**
   a. Mark 12:30-31
   b. Matthew 19
   c. Ephesians 5:22
   d. 1 Peter 3:7
   e. Ephesians 5:28-29
   f. Mark 10:7-8
   g. 1 Corinthians 7:5
   h. Matthew 19
   i. Genesis 2
   j. 1 Corinthians 11:3
   k. Ephesians 5:31
   l. Proverbs 24:6
   m. Matthew 19:8-12

5. **Anger Soup**
   a. James 1:19-20
   b. Genesis 1:1
   c. Romans 1:18-20
   d. Romans 12:17-21
   e. Matthew 18:15-17

← Scripture References by Chapter →

    f. Ephesians 4:31
    g. Ecclesiastes 7:9
    h. Proverbs 22:24
    i. Ephesians 6:4

6. **The Weight and Blessing of Children**
    a. Titus 2
    b. Titus 2:6
    c. 1 Corinthians 11:1
    d. John 21:18
    e. Ephesians 4:15
    f. 1 John 3:18

7. **Survive, Alive, or Thrive**
    a. Ecclesiastes 6:7
    b. Matthew 6:34
    c. Colossians 2:6-10
    d. Matthew 6:17–18
    e. Colossians 1:23
    f. Matthew 7:11
    g. Luke 12:18-21
    h. Proverbs 17:24
    i. Psalm 37:4
    j. Colossians 1:28
    k. 2 Corinthians 3:2-3
    l. Romans 2:15
    m. Jeremiah 31:33
    n. John 20:21
    o. Proverbs 16:3

p. Acts 1:8
q. John 20:21
r. Psalm 96:3
s. Matthew 24:14
t. Mark 16:15
u. Romans 1:16

8. **You Should Judge Me**
   a. Matthew 7:4
   b. Romans 2:1
   c. 1 Corinthians 11:32
   d. Luke 15:31-32
   e. Luke 5:32
   f. Romans 5:8
   g. Matthew 5:14-16

9. **Power**
   a. 1 Corinthians 12:15
   b. Genesis 11
   c. 2 Corinthians 1:21-22
   d. 1 Peter 2:9-10
   e. Psalm 119:7
   f. 2 Corinthians 6:1
   g. James 2:18
   h. Hebrews 11:6
   i. 1 Corinthians 3:9

10. **Mom, the Unicorn is Acting Weird**
    a. Romans 1:20

← Scripture References by Chapter →

b. Revelation 4:6-8
c. Genesis 1:20-27
d. Revelation 4
e. Genesis 2:7
f. 1 John
g. John 24:16
h. Romans 8:26
i. Romans 8:27
j. Acts 2
k. Matthew 22:29
l. Romans 8:34
m. Hebrews 4:15-16
n. John 14:26
o. Leviticus 19:31
p. Revelation 12:9
q. Hebrews 1:14
r. Luke 1:11
s. Hebrews 13:2
t. 1 John 4:2-3
u. Colossians 2:9
v. 1 Corinthians 6:3
w. Luke 2:9-10
x. Matthew 1:20-21
y. Acts 27:23-25
z. Colossians 1:15

11. **You Need There to Be A God**
    a. Ecclesiastes 1:4

b. Philippians 3:8
c. Numbers 23:19
d. Revelations 10:4
e. Romans 12:11
f. Psalm 96:4-5
g. John 10:34
h. Colossians 1: 15-17
i. John 14:16
j. Ezekiel 8:14-15
k. Ezekiel 8:16
l. Exodus 20:3
m. Matthew 22:37
n. Psalm 97:9
o. 1 John 4:16
p. Hebrews 5
q. Hebrews 6:17
r. Colossians 1:23
s. Hebrews 6:16-20
t. Luke 6:27
u. Luke 6:30
v. Job 1:21
w. Luke 6
x. James 1:5

12. **Truth (Part 2) the Harsh Lesson**
    a. John 8:44
    b. 1 John 3:8
    c. Hebrews 10:16

← Scripture References by Chapter →

d. Hebrews 10:29
e. Psalm 25:5
f. 1 Timothy 4:6
g. 1 Timothy 4:7
h. 2 Timothy 2:15
i. John 3:16

ISBN: 978-1-7378981-2-2 (paperback)

Visit MarcusLDavis.com
Publisher Marcus1Media.com

www.ingramcontent.com/pod-product-compliance
Lightning Source LLC
Chambersburg PA
CBHW032126090426
42743CB00007B/486